Praise for *Finding God Along the Way*

"A long hike provides space for meditation and epiphanies, and this book provides them on every page, together with the everyday challenges of blisters, variable weather, and quirky but delightful international companions. Christine's observations will illuminate your own walk—halfway around the world or in your own backyard."

Senator Tim Kaine, US Senator from Virginia and author of *Walk, Ride, Paddle*

"Christine catches the spirit of the pilgrimage, living the full experience in her own body and soul and bringing an open mind to both the obstacles and wonders that pilgrims may encounter along the Way."

José Luis Iriberri, SJ, Director, Office of the Ignatian Camino

"In this beautifully written book, Eberle encourages readers to risk what it means to step into the unknown each day, putting the Camino experience within every person's reach."

Paula D'Arcy, author of *Waking Up to This Day* and *Stars at Night*

"A great read! Christine has distilled the essence of pilgrimage and integrated Ignatian Spirituality into a wonderfully engaging narrative. With a lovely light touch she manages to capture the daily struggles and challenges that make for the essential inner journey that mirrors the outer journey in Ignatian Spain. This book beautifully illustrates Ignatian themes of trust, freedom, and listening to the Spirit."

Brendan McManus, SJ, Camino Guide, Spiritual Director, and Author

"Christine Marie Eberle's *Finding God Along the Way* felt like an unexpected, long catch up with your best friend on a Sunday afternoon. I found myself in tears as I read the beginning question, 'Do you want to go for a walk with me?' and they came often as I read so many relatable struggles wrapped in countless encouraging words and prayers."

Katie (Haseltine) Mullin, Author of *All the Things: A 30 Day Guide to Experiencing God's Presence in the Prayer of Examen*

"With warmth, humor, and a voracious eye for detail, Eberle masterfully weaves stories that transport us to the land of St. Ignatius while keeping us grounded in the spiritual reality of our own present lives. While we can't all hop a flight to Spain, we can all journey deeper into those hidden recesses of our souls, where God waits with delight. If you're looking for an adventure into the soul, this is your book."

Eric A. Clayton, Author of *My Life with the Jedi* and *Cannonball Moments*

"The questions Eberle asks at the end of each reflection remind me that life is a pilgrimage, and that whether I travel through Spain or my own backyard, it is the same God who is leading the way."

⸱n M. Garrido, Associate Professor of Homiletics at Aquinas Institute of Theology, St. Louis, MO

"An inviting book that artfully weaves together Christine's pilgrimage with the history of Ignatius and the author's own deep reflection on what she learned about herself—and her God. The scriptures she shares and the prompts for our own reflection are icing on the cake. You will find much to savor in this book."

Jeff Crosby, Author of *The Language of the Soul:*
Meeting God in the Longings of Our Hearts

"Christine Eberle is not only an experienced, funny, and wise spiritual guide. She's also a great storyteller. The rhythm of this book—action, reflection, action, reflection—is the heart of pilgrimage and of Ignatian spirituality itself."

Jonathan Malesic, Author of *The End of Burnout:*
Why Work Drains Us and How to Build Better Lives

"What a delight to journey along the Ignatian Camino with Christine Eberle as our wise and thoughtful guide! Scripture, story, and Ignatian principles are woven together in a meditative and inspiring guide not only for those making a literal pilgrimage, but for all of us who lace up our shoes each morning to walk through the holy and challenging terrain of our own lives."

Cameron Bellm, Author of *The Sacrament of Paying Attention: Contemplative*
Practices for Restoring Sacred Human Communion (Eerdmans, Fall 2025)

"With her trademark tongue-in-cheek wit and relentless honesty, Eberle crafts both an entertaining and accessible memoir and a guidebook for meditating on life's most important questions. At turns harrowing and joyous, this is a book that lets the reader inhabit each step of an uplifting and transformative odyssey."

David W. Burns, Author of *Heart of Stone* (Book One of *The Medusa Chronicles*)

"With profound insight, vulnerability, and humor, Eberle invites readers to journey alongside her as she reflects on the modern-day relevance of Ignatian Spirituality, and its capability—like pilgrimage—to transform our hearts, our minds, and our perspectives."

Jennifer Sawyer, Editor-in-Chief of Busted Halo

"At first glance, this is a book about how extraordinary circumstances supercharged one woman's spiritual growth. Dig deeper, and it's really about how ordinary life can also reveal our own opportunities to grow with God."

Elizabeth Grace Matthew, EdD, Regular opinion contributor at "The Hill"
and Catholic mother of four

Wisdom from the
Ignatian Camino
for Life at Home

Finding
GOD
Along
the
Way

Christine Marie Eberle

PARACLETE PRESS
Brewster, Massachusetts

2025 First Printing

Finding God Along the Way: Wisdom from the Ignatian Camino for Life at Home

ISBN 978-1-64060-989-1

Text copyright © 2025 by Christine Marie Eberle

The Paraclete Press name and logo (dove on cross) are trademarks of Paraclete Press.

Map on page 11 courtesy of José Luis Iriberri, SJ

Library of Congress Cataloging-in-Publication Data
Names: Eberle, Christine Marie, 1965- author.
Title: Finding God along the way : wisdom from the Ignatian Camino for life
  at home / Christine Marie Eberle.
Description: Brewster, Massachusetts : Paraclete Press, [2025] | Summary:
  "Eberle invites readers to journey alongside her as she treks 300 miles
  in the footsteps of St. Ignatius of Loyola. Her reflections offer the
  possibility of transforming our hearts and minds"-- Provided by
  publisher.
Identifiers: LCCN 2024036895 (print) | LCCN 2024036896 (ebook) | ISBN
  9781640609891 (trade paperback) | ISBN 9781640609907 (epub)
Subjects: LCSH: Spiritual life--Catholic Church. | Ignatius, of Loyola,
  Saint, 1491-1556. | Christian pilgrims and pilgrimages--Spain. | Eberle,
  Christine Marie, 1965-
Classification: LCC BX2350 .E24 2025 (print) | LCC BX2350 (ebook) | DDC
  263/.042461--dc23/eng/20240905
LC record available at https://lccn.loc.gov/2024036895
LC ebook record available at https://lccn.loc.gov/2024036896

10 9 8 7 6 5 4 3 2 1

Published by Paraclete Press
Brewster, Massachusetts
www.paracletepress.com

Printed in the United States of America

For José Luis Iriberri, SJ, who is changing the world one pilgrimage at a time.

For my companions on the journey:
Mama Jane, Tony, Karen, Dave, Betsy, Charlie, Beth-Anne, Canada Jane, Jim, Veronica, Louise, Kathy, Ana, Rose, Carmen, Mary, Pete, Liz, Bette, Ann, both Pats, and Mary Jo.

And for Porter, who has my hand and my heart to the end of the road.

Contents

The Light of a Story

In the fall of 2022, I spent four weeks on the Ignatian Camino—a three-hundred-mile walking route across northeastern Spain. This pilgrimage is one of the best and hardest things I've ever done. I abandoned my familiar surroundings, pushed myself to hike many miles each day over varied terrain in the company of people I'd just met, and spent the first two hours of every walk in prayerful silence.

It sounds extraordinary, and on one level, it was. And yet, how often have you heard the phrase *life is a journey*? For one month, I simply put that metaphor into practice, trusting the physical walk to inform my spiritual one.

This is where our paths converge. As I'm sure you've experienced, life can take us out of our comfort zone at a moment's notice. How do we get through it? By putting one foot in front of the other for as long as it takes. Prayer helps, as do good companions.

However, pilgrimage is not just about perseverance. It is a quest for transformation. As Paul Elie wrote in *The Life You Save May Be Your Own*:

> A pilgrimage is a journey undertaken in the light of a story. A great event has happened; the pilgrim hears the reports and goes in search of the evidence, aspiring to be an eyewitness. The pilgrim seeks not only to confirm the experience of others firsthand but to be changed by the experience.
>
> Pilgrims often make the journey in company, but each must be changed individually; they must see for themselves, each with his or her own eyes. And as they return to ordinary life, the pilgrims must tell others what they saw, recasting the story in their own terms.

My journey was undertaken in the light of the story of Ignatius of Loyola, a man I've admired since my undergraduate days at Saint Joseph's University. Often called the "pilgrim saint," Ignatius—following a battlefield injury, painful recovery, and spiritual awakening—traveled in 1522 from his home in the Basque region of Spain to the Benedictine monastery of Montserrat and then the nearby city of Manresa, where he remained for eleven months. Thus began the world-changing story of the man who would go on to found the Society of Jesus (the Jesuits). His were the steps we would retrace.

I made this journey in the company of twenty-four women and men gathered by the Ignatian Volunteer Corps. A nationwide organization founded and sponsored by Jesuits, IVC matches individuals over fifty in long-term volunteer placements, supporting service corps members with a program of spiritual formation in community. A pilgrimage for members and friends of IVC along the *Camino Ignaciano*—the Ignatian Camino—was part of the organization's twenty-fifth anniversary celebration.

When people hear the word "Camino," they usually think of the *Camino de Santiago*—the Way of Saint James—a more famous and ancient route than the one we took. I chose the lesser-known pilgrimage because I wanted to walk the Way of Saint Ignatius: to learn from his experience and be changed by my own. This desire sang in the hearts of my companions as well. As each of us returned to ordinary life, we searched for adequate ways to share what we had experienced and learned. This book is my attempt.

I am convinced that the wisdom of the Ignatian Camino is not just for those with the resources to fly to Spain, lace up their boots, and hit the road. It is *everyday* wisdom, useful whether or not your life is marked by good health, financial freedom, or job flexibility. Like all wisdom, it needs to be savored, so I would encourage you not to race through the book. Every insight is the fruit of hours of walking, pondering, praying, and journaling. If something rings a bell for you, go ahead and pause (or at least flag it for later). My deepest desire is that you will join me on this road and allow my journey to shed light on yours. To that end, I've added a few questions for reflection at the end of each chapter.

I pray that you will recognize your own pilgrim heart in these pages—and discover new ways to follow where it leads.

Map of the Pilgrimage Route

PRE-AMBLE

AUGUST 2019 ~ OCTOBER 2022

CHAPTER ONE

Delay

For there is still a vision for the appointed time . . .
If it seems to tarry, wait for it; it will surely come, it will not delay.

—Habakkuk 2:3 (NRSVCE)

On an October evening in 2022, fifteen pilgrims still trying to remember each other's names shifted anxiously in a circle of hard plastic chairs, eyes trained on our fearless Jesuit guide. The fluorescent-lit conference room's unadorned walls gave no hint that we were in the shadow of the tower house of Loyola—the long-envisioned starting point of our grand adventure.

The youngest of us was fifty-five, the oldest seventy-nine. We were ten women and five men, hailing from across the United States as well as Canada, Australia, and Malaysia. The group included couples, widows, singles, and married folks traveling solo. Some were old friends; others knew no one. Although many were part of the Ignatian Volunteer Corps, the rest were drawn simply by their love of Ignatian spirituality. Seventeen days and some two hundred miles later, ten more people would be joining us for the final hundred miles of our journey.

My own Camino story had already been four years in the making. In 2018, I had published my first book and was getting ready to transition from a career in college campus ministry to a freelance existence. For the first time in my life, my time was about to be my own. It was the best possible moment for Mary McGinnity, President and CEO of IVC, to ask if I'd be interested in helping her plan a pilgrimage.

Mary had been longing to offer this to the IVC community from the moment she met the Ignatian Camino's director (and aforementioned fearless guide), Fr. José Luis Iriberri, SJ. The Spanish Jesuit priest was in the United States for a publicity tour, effervescent in his description of the transformative power of pilgrimage. Mary knew, however, that the route from big idea to accomplished endeavor inevitably involves a long slog through a muddy field of details.

That's where I came in.

I'd been a friend of IVC for years. My brother, Stephen, was on the national staff, and my beloved, Porter, was an Ignatian volunteer at Sanctuary Farm in Philadelphia. I'd given retreats for volunteers, staff, and board members. Mary had a good grasp of my skill set, and I had a deep fondness for the organization. When she asked, my answer was a resounding *yes*.

Within IVC, the idea flared and faltered until August of 2019, when Mary finally gave us the green light to secure dates for a fall 2020 Camino.

Yup.

Fall of 2020.

By the time COVID-19 began tripping the circuit breakers of plans throughout the world, Stephen and I had advertised the Camino and gathered our cohort. In late March, we sent an email to the pilgrims announcing our intention to press on "with guarded optimism." On April 22, Porter and I stepped out in faith and *bought airline tickets.* (Clearly, we had not grasped the implications of this pandemic!)

When would travel be possible again? We rebooked for the spring of 2021 then quickly punted to fall, never imagining that a full year's postponement would be insufficient. When even that plan was revealed as folly, I wrote to Fr. José to reschedule the IVC Camino for a third time, two years and one month after our original travel dates.

The pilgrimage I made in 2022 is not the one I would have had in 2020. So much had changed in two years. The world had endured a frightening pandemic and our country a fraught presidential election, with ripple effects at every level of society, church, and family. I'd grown my freelance career, published a second book, and was ready to ask new questions about life and ministry. Even my body was different—two years farther into middle age. From the perspective of pilgrimage, none of this was better or worse; it was just real. The particular circumstances of my life at that time would be the raw material God used for the work of transformation.

The Camino's participants had shifted as well. Several from the original roster persisted through every rescheduling—members of the IVC community as well as other "friends of Ignatius" whom Fr. José had introduced to our group. Others had lost their passion for travel during the pandemic or suffered physical setbacks; tragically, one service corps member died before she could realize her dream of making the Camino. On the other hand, the delay made it possible for others to join us: those whose lives had acquired more freedom in the wake of the virus, as well as those who had joined IVC after the initial recruitment window closed.

Altogether, fifty-seven individuals expressed interest in the Camino—any one of whom would have changed our dynamic. Why were these twenty-five souls brought together in the end? God only knows. I say this with no rhetorical flourish; as you will read in the pages to come, our encounters with one another were as impactful as anything else we experienced on the journey. *Surely, God had a hand in this,* I muse (mentally paraphrasing a line from Mary Oliver's poem "Heavy").

The story of our pilgrimage could be told from twenty-six perspectives, counting Fr. José's, yet I can tell it faithfully from only my own. (If that means you're about to read more about blister care than you ever wanted to know, I do apologize.) I have tried to incorporate the memories and musings of my companions wherever possible, always with their explicit approval.

I'm getting ahead of myself, though. Before the strangers in those plastic chairs became my companions—before these (now) dear ones were any more to me than names on a spreadsheet and faces on a Zoom screen—God was at work, preparing me for the Way.

What has changed for you in the past few years? At the beginning of your journey through this book, pause to take stock of the particular circumstances of your life today, recognizing that this is precisely where you will find God.

CHAPTER TWO

Will You Go for a Walk with Me?

Come, let us go up to the LORD's mountain,
to the house of the God of Jacob,
That he may instruct us in his ways,
and we may walk in his paths.

—Isaiah 2:3 (NABRE)

Mary's invitation to help organize the Camino arrived while three other things were happening: it was my final year as a college campus minister; I was firing up a freelance career with the launch of my first book, and my legs had stopped working. If this sounds dramatic, that's because it was.

For no reason that was ever diagnosed, pain that started in one knee had spread throughout my lower extremities, making my legs both stiff and unreliable. Over the course of a few months, I had gone from running around campus to needing a cane. An assortment of tests revealed nothing; a variety of specialists remained clueless.

Eventually, I got better—mostly. (My knees still don't bend like they used to.) The only explanation I have for my temporary disability is that sometimes the body puts its foot down—a lesson to which I would return on the Camino. I'd always considered myself a multitasker, pridefully cramming efficient action into every nook and cranny of my calendar. But this time, I had taken on too much. I'd thought it was manageable to spend "just one year" as Director of Campus Ministry while becoming a retreat facilitator and freelance writer with a book in the world. I was wrong.

In *The White Album,* Joan Didion described migraines as her body's response to the "guerrilla wars" of her life. Like Didion's headaches forcing her into a darkened room with an ice pack, my legs were shouting that I needed to sit down.

Things had begun improving but were not yet resolved when my brother first mentioned the pilgrimage. The *Camino de Santiago* had been on my theoretical bucket list for a good decade, but I'd never heard of the Ignatian Camino. As a person formed by two Jesuit universities and decades of Ignatian retreats, however, I found the idea compelling. I'd known the story of the eventual saint's pilgrimage since college; the chance to visit places I'd only seen in my imagination was irresistible. (I also suspect I viewed organizing a pilgrimage as a way to add structure to the alarmingly wide-open year to come.) As soon as Mary posed her question, I was in.

And yet, my legs were still not working terribly well. How was I even considering a three-hundred-mile hike? I was nowhere as brave as Ignatius, who made the journey after a devastating leg injury. Praying with this conundrum, I suddenly sensed a new invitation in my spirit. Although I try not to be one of those religious writers who wigs you out by using language like "And then Jesus said," that's what it felt like. A single sentence materialized amid my prayerful fussing: *"Do you want to go for a walk with me?"*

The question cut through my angst, leaving my spirit settled. *Do I want to go for a walk with you, Lord? Yes. Yes, I do.*

Though I would find plenty of other things to worry about during our preparatory months-turned-years, that certitude never left me. And it was, in the end, what it felt like to be on the Ignatian Camino.

No matter what any given day held, I knew I was going for a walk with God.

Do you have a favorite place to walk? What makes it special? Can you imagine walking with God there, speaking from the heart as you would with a good friend? If you are someone for whom walking is painful or even impossible, I invite you to embrace the metaphor anyway, listening for God's invitation to move together—however slowly—throughout your day.

CHAPTER THREE

In the Autumn of Life

For everything there is a season,
and a time for every matter under heaven.

—Ecclesiastes 3:1 (NRSVCE)

The first thing we had to decide was when to go. What season of the year is best for a Camino? Though summer's too hot and winter's too cold, spring and fall each have their advantages, so I drew up a list of pros and cons. If we walked in spring, we'd enjoy up to fourteen hours of daylight, which would be lovely, but we'd have to do our long training walks in winter, which would not. If we walked in fall, we could train in summer (problematic in its own way), but the days would be short; sometimes we'd have to set out in darkness or reach our destination with the setting sun. (To complicate matters further, training weather would be reversed for our pilgrims from the southern hemisphere.)

In the end, the pandemic chose for us, but fall turned out to be the perfect season for an Ignatian Volunteer Corps Camino. IVC members are age "fifty and better" . . . some *much* better. We are a community in the autumn of life; the metaphor alone made October an ideal month for our journey. Through the Camino, we embodied an essential quest of the Corps: to grow closer to God in our "encore years," always listening, as St. Ignatius did, for divine invitations.

An essential part of our pilgrimage was the two hours we would spend in silence each day, praying with material from the *Spiritual Exercises*. Organized into four thematic weeks (which unfold over varied amounts of time, depending on the individual), this retreat is the cornerstone of Ignatian spirituality. The saint envisioned the *Exercises* as an aid to discernment, designed to liberate the retreatants from the influence of any "inordinate attachment."

Often, people make this retreat on the brink of a major decision: Jesuits approaching vows, for example, or someone contemplating a significant life change. Turning points, however, are not reserved for the young. In the autumn of life, what decisions did we face? What inordinate attachments threatened our freedom to make them? The particulars varied, but we were all of an age when *time*, never infinite, was clearly finite. We had to ask ourselves: How was God calling us to serve the world in our remaining years? How would we spend our limited strength, health, and resources? These are relevant questions at any age, but they are particularly potent in autumn. To paraphrase Mary Oliver again, we had to ask ourselves: What were we going to *have done* with our one wild and precious life?

The metaphor did not disappoint. Together, we pondered the urgencies of the season. We opened ourselves to a fresh adventure at an age when we could easily grow set in our ways. We savored broad vistas at a time when the horizon could be narrowing. Like trees shedding their leaves, we let go of what was not essential in order to travel unencumbered. In the spirit of the Ignatian Volunteer Corps, we set out—in the autumn of the year and the autumn of our lives—to discover what would come next.

What season of life are you in? What are its unique gifts? Can you embrace those gifts, even as you lament the loss of seasons past or fear the season to come?

CHAPTER FOUR

Background Music

*Your word is a lamp to my feet
and a light to my path.*

—Psalm 119:105 (NRSVCE)

When does a pilgrimage begin? It's not when you strap on your backpack, unfold your hiking poles, and set your foot on the path. It's not when you lock your front door, suitcase in hand, to leave for the airport. It's not even when you book—or rebook—your flight. A pilgrimage begins, quite simply, the moment you commit to it. The Way reaches out to you, shifting your attention and actions from afar. Did you ever buy a car and suddenly begin seeing that model everywhere? The highways haven't been flooded by one automobile; the change is in your noticing.

As soon as I said yes to the Camino, it became the background music of my days, altering my habits as well as my perceptions. I started walking with my backpack to a mom-and-pop grocery store a mile away instead of driving to the supermarket. If I commenced a walk and discovered that my socks were scrunchy or my layers not quite right for the temperature, I would shrug and keep going rather than circling back to get changed. I began paying attention to my reliance on technology. Did I really need to have a podcast playing during every walk, or could I listen to my thoughts instead?

Long before I set foot in Spain, the Camino had become a conversation partner, gently weighing in on my everyday decisions and attitudes. Nevertheless, I was dogged by the nagging fear that I wouldn't be making a *real* Camino. Why? Because I'd be doing it with support.

In my imagination, Camino-making pilgrims carried everything on their backs, relied on guidebooks and signposts for directions, and took their chances with lodging each night—elements dramatically portrayed in Martin Sheen's movie *The Way*. That was the pure experience, the "real" pilgrimage, yes?

When I told people I was making a Camino, I could tell from their questions that they were using that idealized image as a yardstick. While no one accused me of cheating (except in jest), I'll confess it's how I felt before I got there. But as much as I loved *The Way*, I knew myself too well to try to replicate it. There was no age at which I could have carried twenty percent of my body weight (REI's recommended max) on my shoulders. I am too visually unobservant to put my faith in signposts and travel markings. And not knowing where or if I'd find a bed for the night would have cast too long a shadow of anxiety across each day.

Instead, IVC put the details of our journey in the hands of Fr. José, who left nothing to chance except that which he couldn't control (which still was plenty). He measured the distances between towns, found modest accommodations at walkable intervals, then added occasional bus or train segments to bridge the gaps. He contracted with a driver in each region to transport our suitcases every morning, leaving us to carry only what we needed for the hike. He figured out each meal: making restaurant reservations, ordering pickup sandwiches via WhatsApp, or identifying grocery stores where we could purchase food for the next day.

By the standards of *The Way*, we'd be total slackers. But why were those the standards? In my journal, I wrote, *Why must there be a right and wrong way to do this? With whom am I in competition? It's a pilgrimage—a spiritual journey. The important thing is to be open to what comes.*

There was much fruitful ground, I realized, between the extremes of total uncertainty and total security. Our Camino would have its share of question marks, physical challenges, and detours from personal comfort zones. In each place of discomfort, I would encounter God in a new way. I didn't need to rough it like a gap-year teenager backpacking around Europe. Even if I could have pulled that off, the heroics would have shifted my focus from where it belonged: I needed to embrace the uncertainty, appreciate the security, and be present to God, to myself, and to my traveling companions.

Even while it lived only in my imagination, the Ignatian Way was a good conversation partner. Now that it lives only in my memory, the pilgrimage continues to speak.

I hope the conversation never ends.

———————————

Many things in our lives can become "conversation partners"—present like background music, shaping our thoughts, feelings, and choices. What are yours? Are they yielding fruitful conversations? If not, how might you change the topic?

CHAPTER FIVE

Worrying

*Can any of you by worrying
add a single moment to your life-span?*

—Matthew 6:27 (NABRE)

Most sentences that begin with *'What if . . .'* are probably from the evil spirit." Susan Bowers Baker, my spiritual director, offered me this bit of wisdom over twenty years ago. If I were the sort of person to get a tattoo, I would have inked it on the back of my hand for the run-up to the Camino, so frequently did I start sentences with those two treacherous words.

Trying to fall asleep at night, my brain would serve up a tapas platter of worst-case scenarios. *What if your back goes out? What if Porter's cancer resurfaces? What if one of you gets COVID and can't fly? What if someone you love becomes critically ill before you leave, or dies while you're away?*

This line of thinking was a total waste of brain space. Except in the rare instances when there was something I could do to ward off disaster—like staying faithful to my Pilates lessons so my back wouldn't go out—the only answer to most of my late-night what-ifs was the one given to St. Paul in 2 Corinthians: "My grace is sufficient for you."

Susan and I talked a lot about grace in our last session before I left for Spain. "We can't live in the 'what-ifs' because we haven't been given the grace to meet them yet," she said, insisting that any divine assistance I required would be there when I needed it—but no sooner. And I knew she was right; I'd experienced that sort of rising-to-meet-me grace before.

I had even experienced it (now that I thought about it) in relation to one of my what-ifs. During COVID, Porter's bladder cancer *had* resurfaced, requiring him to be on monthly chemo throughout 2022— yet the Camino would be taking us out of the country for five weeks. In late summer, we met with two of his nurses to book the next several rounds of treatment. Those good women twisted themselves into pretzels trying to schedule a series of infusions that would meet the protocols for minimum and maximum intervals while leapfrogging over our travels.

Looking at Chris's and Jenny's scrunched faces peering at their calendars and scribbled notes, I braced myself for them to swivel around, hands on hips, and say, "Do you understand that he has *cancer*?" But they never did. Patiently, they figured it out. When I thanked them profusely for all the time and trouble, they waved me off, saying, "We understand cancer's only one part of your life."

What can I say? Sometimes the grace that rises to meet you is wearing scrubs.

A less dire but more itchy set of worries involved creature comforts. *What if I can't sleep without listening to the radio? What if I can't sleep well without my own pillow? What if I can't find reliable morning coffee? What if I can't find a reliable bathroom ten minutes after morning coffee? What if I have to relieve myself in the woods—and how do stay hydrated if I'm not willing to?*

Again, the only dilemmas on that list worth thinking about were the ones that allowed me to take productive action. I purchased a travel pillow and hydration tablets. I downloaded the audiobook of *Little Women* so I could listen to something pleasant but not Wi-Fi dependent as I fell asleep. Having gotten hooked on morning joe in *eighth grade,* I made room in my luggage for a jar of instant coffee, a travel mug, and an immersion heater.

To be clear: I wish I were a person who did not need these things. Once on the Camino, I regarded with envy the compact suitcases of savvy travelers who had not brought coffee paraphernalia or compressible pillows. But what fascinates me, in retrospect, are the things I let go of that could have used a little actionable worry. Despite having three years to prepare and investing a lot of research into selecting the proper *socks*, I ran out of time to figure out my shoes. I knew the excellent hiking boots and supportive sneakers I'd bought were causing me trouble, but I didn't know what to do except buy a good pair of orthotics and assume I'd deal with it.

Similarly, despite owning a detailed guidebook that charted every kilometer of our walk—complete with heights of ascent and descent—I never did the math and found similar hiking routes at home to practice on. Friends knitted their brows and asked if I was training, and I confessed that I really was not. I told them that, despite having been enthusiastic about it during Year One, there was something about the repeated postponement that had sapped my motivation to train. It would just have to be okay, I shrugged.

My decision to focus more on my coffee than my feet remains mystifying. But one thing was clear: much of my worry was a smoke screen—an attempt to control what I could in the face of everything that was profoundly unknowable. In my journal, I wrote, *I know that the physical challenges will be an external manifestation of spiritual ones, but I don't know how to prepare for that other than to acknowledge it.*

The only remedy was to begin.

_____

What "what-ifs" are plaguing you today? Are they "actionable worries" or simply a paralyzing smoke screen? If the former, what action can you take? If the latter, how might you invite the gentle breeze of God's Holy Spirit to blow that smoke away so you can see more clearly?

CHAPTER SIX

The Limits of Perfection

For by grace you have been saved through faith,
and this is not your own doing; it is the gift of God.

—Ephesians 2:8 (NRSVCE)

When I quit my day job, one of my great desires was to stop being in charge of things. Though I loved ministry, I no longer wanted to tackle enormous projects with four hundred moving parts. I longed to be responsible for no one but myself—and yet, I was not immune to the siren call of an ambitious undertaking. Though Mary had only invited me to *help* plan it, I quickly decided that the only way to guarantee the pilgrimage happened would be to take charge.

Throughout my career, my leadership had been both fueled and frustrated by perfectionism and its twin sister, control. This would be true for the Camino as well. Fortunately, I'd had the good sense to ask my brother to co-coordinate, and we easily divided responsibilities according to our gifts and interests. Generally, Stephen dealt with in-house and financial matters, while I became the point person for communication with prospective pilgrims and the Office of the Ignatian Camino.

I'm not sure why I decided I should be the only person interacting with Fr. José; certainly, he had never set that rule. But I sensed that it would be helpful to have a single channel for questions and requests. I felt a tremendous responsibility to make good decisions and provide everyone with all the information they needed while bothering this busy priest as little as possible. Like most things in my leadership history, this was both helpful and taxing.

Although each traveler was responsible for booking their own flight to Spain, one of the things I took upon myself was figuring out how to get us to Loyola itself. In 2019, Fr. José had directed me to a morning train that would take us from Barcelona to San Sebastian, thirty miles from Loyola. From there, we could catch a bus that would get us to the retreat house in time for our evening orientation meeting.

Accordingly—three years later—I encouraged everyone to fly into Barcelona and recommended a hotel right across the street from the train station. All but one person went along with my scheme, buying their tickets and booking their rooms. Two months before the trip, when folks began pressing me for the particulars of how we were getting to Loyola, I looked at the train schedule again.

Uh-oh.

The morning train from Barcelona to San Sebastian had been canceled during COVID and never rescheduled. Feeling my stomach drop, I frantically began researching other options. Surely, there was another train or bus that would get us there on time, right? Wrong. Loyola was three hundred and sixty-five miles away, on the far side of a couple of mountains. The only way to take public transportation and be in place for an early evening meeting would be to leave Barcelona the day before.

I really did not want to dump this crisis in Fr. José's lap, but I had no choice. I had managed to identify a few charter bus companies that might be able to take us door-to-door, but I'd reached the limits of what I trusted myself to do in a foreign language from the other side of the pond. His response caught me by surprise. *Oh, don't bother with a long, boring ride,* he replied. *Just hop a flight to Bilbao and take the bus from there; that's what I always do.*

Just hop a flight to Bilbao. *Just?* On my advice, people were going to be flying into Barcelona and dragging their luggage to a hotel in the shadow of the train station. Now I was supposed to tell them to go back to the airport the next morning and board a tiny (I supposed) plane to an obscure (I imagined) *other* airport?

I did not want to fly to Bilbao. I did not want to tell anyone else they needed to fly to Bilbao. I did not want to schlep luggage through the subway again, risking missed connections or misplaced pilgrims. When I finally reached Barcelona, I wanted to lay down my burdens, step on a coach, hand the proverbial reins to Fr. José, and watch the scenery unfold in real time as we traced our route backwards over the terrain we were about to walk.

I threw myself on the priest's mercy and he arranged for Carlos Perez, his Basque-region luggage transport guy, to drive all the way to

Barcelona to pick us up and deliver us to the doorstep of our residence in Loyola. I put the whole thing on my credit card and asked the pilgrims to reimburse me, which they gladly did. (Turns out they didn't want to fly to Bilbao either.)

Somewhere in those frantic hours of planning and re-planning, I could feel Fr. José shaking his head as he typed. *Why did you not tell these people to meet you in Loyola?*

Why indeed? It's where the itinerary began; any organizing prior to that was just raising my hand for more work. But I couldn't help myself; it felt like the right thing to do—so, while I was at it, I found a restaurant in Barcelona where the pilgrims could share a meal the night before departure. And selected a menu. And took everyone's dinner orders, a full month out.

The morning after we resolved the transportation crisis, I went for a long walk and prayed about it. Though the logistical problem had needed solving, my distress felt disproportionate. What buttons had been pushed? I realized that this felt similar to the experience of taking college students on service trips to Mexico City, where my role as an imperfect translator sometimes led to comic misunderstandings that did not feel the least bit funny at the time. It also reminded me of the many large retreats and conferences I had run—quite capably—when the minor dissatisfactions of a few people stranded me emotionally on islands of failure in a sea of success.

As I prayed, a new image came to mind. Jesus tucked my hair behind my ear and said, "Maybe we do it differently this time?" After the walk, in my journal I wrote, *Oh, yes, Lord. Yes, if at all possible! These are grownups with a spirit for travel. They will be okay.*

As I pondered how I could have handled the situation better, I remembered something a wise friend had told me years ago: you can't use your personality to solve problems created *by* your personality. In other words, I couldn't *try harder* to be less of a perfectionist.

What I could do, however, was release the illusion of control. Like a mosaic artist, God was the one piecing together this pilgrimage, using each person's distinctive shape and rough edges to create something beautiful. Why should I be exempt? On the Camino, grace would work *through*—not despite—my imperfections, arriving when I needed it most. That's what St. Paul was getting at when he said that God's power is "made perfect in weakness" (2 Cor. 12:9, NABRE). I just couldn't see it yet.

Packing lightly, I mused, was not only about the luggage. It was also about the baggage.

What roles do perfectionism and control play in your life? Can you imagine desiring to live differently? Talk to God about this.

CHAPTER SEVEN

Commissionings

Therefore, since we are surrounded by so great a cloud of witnesses,
let us rid ourselves of every burden and sin that clings to us
and persevere in running the race that lies before us.

—Hebrews 12:1–2 (NABRE)

On the last Monday in September, IVC held a commissioning ceremony via Zoom, led by board member Fr. Jim Fleming, SJ. Most of the pilgrims were able to be present, along with eighty-some family and friends. We listened to Paul Elie's words about pilgrimage and the account in Luke's Gospel about the disciples on the road to Emmaus, followed by an excerpt from a Jan Richardson blessing:

So open your heart
to these shimmering hours
by which your path
is made.

Open your eyes
to the light that shines
on what you will need
to see.

Open your hands
to those who go with you,
those seen
and those known only
by their blessing, their benediction
of the road that is
your own.

Then Fr. Jim posed three questions:

- Will you open your heart to the Ignatian Camino, with all its promise and uncertainty: surrendering your hopes and dreams for this experience so that you may find God in all you encounter along the Way?
- Will you open your eyes to your own physical, emotional, and spiritual well-being: equipping yourselves with the fruits of God's Holy Spirit—love, joy, peace, patience, kindness, generosity, faithfulness, gentleness, and self-control?
- Will you open your hands to care for your companions on the journey: supporting, encouraging, and listening to each other, and gifting one another with the silence and spaciousness needed to draw close to the Divine?

Though we had barely an inkling how much each promise would be tested, the group responded enthusiastically: *We will! We will! We will!*

Before the webinar concluded, we offered ways for people to accompany us. The first was easy. Everyone was already registered for email updates entitled "Dispatches from the Camino," and they also could follow us on social media. My job would be to make sure IVC's communication manager had enough material to keep the feed interesting. The second way required a bit more thought. We invited the community to send prayer intentions for us to carry as we walked.

More than sixty requests flooded in. As I collated them to fit on one piece of paper, I was touched by the vulnerability people shared: asking our prayers for their troubled children and grandchildren, for loved ones with cancer, for friends nearing the end of their lives. They shared their emotional and professional struggles and offered prayers for our protection and transformation. It was moving to realize that so many people would be following our journey, and that we would be carrying their tender concerns with us as we walked. I printed two copies of the document and slipped them into my travel wallet.

The day before we flew to Spain, Porter and I went to Mass at our parish. After Communion, our pastor called us forward to receive a blessing along with Rose and Carmen, two fellow pilgrims who were also St. Vincent's parishioners. Their coming on the Camino was pure serendipity. The first three times it had been scheduled, they had been intrigued yet unavailable; now they were part of the group joining us in Lleida for the final hundred miles.

When people ask how I know Rose, I always say, "Oh, we went to college together," which is true but misleading; we didn't actually know each other at St. Joe's. In our forties, however, I moved into Rose and Carmen's neighborhood and joined the parish in Germantown that they'd called home for decades. As individuals and couples, we soon became friends. They are two of the most thoughtful and generous human beings I know—forever doing something for someone in need. I rarely laugh as hard as I do when hanging out by their fire pit, and some of my best conversations happen during quick after-work walks with Rose. We never have enough time together, so the prospect of two weeks and a hundred miles in their company was like Christmas coming early.

As the four of us stood in the front of church, members of the congregation gathered around us, laying hands on our backs, shoulders, and heads, while my friend Christina—a powerful woman of God who also happens to be our choir's flautist—offered a rousing series of intercessions. In one voice, the people responded: *Buen Camino! Buen Camino! Buen Camino!*

Surrounded by so great a cloud of witnesses, we stepped into the unknown.

If someone asked what they could pray for on your behalf—and really meant it—what intentions would you share? To whose care could you entrust the prayers of your heart today?

CHAPTER EIGHT
Oh, Was That Today?

God has made everything appropriate to its time.

—Ecclesiastes 3:11 (NABRE)

The skies had opened on departure day, so our friend Carolyn chauffeured Porter and me to the neighborhood train station, even though it was only a block away. (We were going to be traveling for eighteen hours; no reason to start with soaking-wet feet, she insisted.) Four trains, one airplane, and two metros later, we were standing in the lobby of the AC Sants Hotel.

We had scheduled our arrival in Barcelona two days earlier than necessary, as a buffer against flight delays and jet lag; this also allowed us to get a bit more post-COVID rest. (Did I mention? We both got COVID—another of my "what-ifs"—just under the wire to fly.) Those two days were like time out of time, helping us transition from one reality to the next.

After a three-hour nap, we wandered into the dining room and encountered a couple who looked familiar. Once we heard their accents, we knew: it was Tony and Jane from Australia! They'd been in Spain for a week already, having taken a pre-Camino walk along the Costa Brava north of Barcelona. Born in South Africa, they had emigrated to Australia decades ago and were serious ultralight hikers—genuine bushwalkers. I had no idea how much I would come to rely on each of them for guidance and support in the days ahead, or how dear they would become to me. We made plans to rendezvous for dinner in a few hours.

Porter and I made our way up the hills of Montjuïc via funicular and cable car, marveling at the views of the city and the harbor, then meandered back down on foot. At a snack shack we lingered in the sun, sharing a bag of chips and sipping Schweppes Limón mixed with pineapple juice—each slightly odd, we decided, but delightful together (much like ourselves). It was hard to fathom that we'd been sitting on a cold train platform in Philadelphia not twenty-four hours earlier!

Dinner with Tony and Jane was wonderful and a bit hysterical, as translation mishaps kept bringing unexpected items to the table. Porter had ordered a glass of Tempranillo; the waiter returned to say they were out of that particular red wine and suggested an alternative, which turned out to be a fizzy white. Jane was hoping for a dish she'd enjoyed the week before—chunky fried potatoes with a spicy red sauce and garlicky mayo—but the waiter delivered roasted potatoes accompanied by an abundance of cheese fondue instead. Later, he walked by carrying the much-ballyhooed item; a frantic inquiry revealed that they were called *patatas bravas*—something we resolved to order whenever we got the chance (and which I've since learned to make). We laughed much, talked more, and ended the day grateful for the chance morning encounter that had made the fun evening possible.

Porter and I continued our exploration of Barcelona the next day, then met the other pilgrims for dinner. Since most of us were staying in the same hotel, we'd agreed to meet downstairs and walk together to *Ocho Patas* ("Eight Legs"—an octopus-themed restaurant!). Matching faces with names was thoroughly amusing; the *Brady Bunch* view on Zoom had not given me an accurate sense of what anyone looked like. After years of seeing their names on a spreadsheet, I found myself asking a bunch of familiar strangers, "Which one are you?" Time after time, I guessed wrong.

At *Ocho Patas*, the dinner was delicious and the conversation convivial. We did what most people do at first encounter—rambled through topics until we identified commonalities. We talked about where we were from, who had spent time in each other's cities, who had made the *Camino de Santiago*, and where else we'd traveled. We swapped pre-retirement occupations, and the ages of our children and grandchildren. (We even got to meet one of those offspring, as Louise's daughter, Eileen—a Barcelona resident since grad school—joined us for dinner.)

Hours later, after licking the last bit of dessert from our spoons, we bid each other goodnight, agreeing to be on the sidewalk with our luggage at 9:45 a.m. to meet Fr. José for the 10:00 bus to Loyola.

In the morning, most folks were punctual—though there were enough stragglers to make me nervous. The luggage itself varied wildly, from carry-on bags so compact it was hard to imagine living out of them for even a week to bulging suitcases with extra items bungeed to the outside. (Lamentably, I found my big red bag near the upper end of that spectrum.)

The appointed rendezvous time came and went, and neither priest nor bus appeared. People began circling back to the restrooms—"go when you can" being a cardinal rule of the Camino already. By 10:15, my vague discomfort had morphed into a bad case of the what-ifs. What if I'd bungled it? What if I'd given Fr. José the wrong address and he was sitting at a *different* hotel, wondering where we were? What if he was trying to reach me, not remembering that I had no cell service in Spain? Jim was one of the few pilgrims who had gotten a local SIM card; eventually, I borrowed his phone and called the office number in Fr. José's email signature, hoping to leave a message or perhaps talk to his secretary.

He answered himself! Haltingly, I explained who I was, and told him we were standing in front of the AC Sants. There was a long, uncomfortable pause. "Oh . . . Was that *today*?" My new friends were watching me closely, puzzled by how little my panic-stricken expression matched my soothing tone. *Well yes, in fact, we've all checked out of our rooms and here we are.* "Okay, give me ten minutes," he said. Then he hung up.

We were now twenty minutes past when I thought I wasn't going to have to be responsible for these people anymore, and instead I was wondering whether we should try to get our rooms back or catch the afternoon train to San Sebastián. Then someone shouted "Look!" as a colorful bus pulled up to the curb and a wiry man with a trim beard and crinkly eyes jumped out.

"Hello, Chris!" Fr. José laughed. (His "office number" had been his mobile, I belatedly realized.) He gave me a big hug, and I pretended to strangle him. Thus began my relationship with the man who would turn out to be one of my favorite people on the planet—eventually.

What cracks me up, besides Fr. José's willingness to have a little fun at my expense, was my willingness to believe he had somehow fuddled the dates—which, if you knew him, you'd know was out of the question. The only appropriate response to his jest should have been "Very funny, Father. Now, where the heck are you? You're late!" (A thing for which he had little tolerance in anyone else, by the way; it must have been the bus driver's fault.)

No matter. He had arrived, and I was off the job. After thirty-eight months of preparation and an extra twenty minutes of worry, the Ignatian Camino had begun.

Think back to your first encounter with a person who is dear to you now. What can you remember? Savor the image of God planting the seeds of your relationship, delighting in knowing what it would look like in full flower.

WEEK ONE:

MOUNTAINS

AZPEITIA ~ LEGAZPI ~ ARANTZAZU ~ EGUINO
~ SANTA CRUZ DE CAMPEZO

The First Principle
and Foundation

During the four weeks of our pilgrimage, we prayed with several key texts from the Spiritual Exercises. *In his "First Principle and Foundation," Ignatius presents the assumptions on which the rest of the Exercises depend. The goal of our life, he proposes, is union with God—who loves us completely, longs to be known, and communicates through the whole of creation and all our experiences. Though God is always near, we alone can determine how deeply we allow God's spirit to penetrate our hearts and guide our actions in loving service. The purpose of the Exercises, then, is to strengthen our ability to open ourselves to God.*

I find the final line here as compelling as it is challenging, proposing a radical detachment from the common indicators of worldly success: I want and I choose what better leads to God's deepening life in me.

IN HIS OWN WORDS:

The goal of our life is to live with God forever.
God, who loves us, gave us life.
Our own response of love allows God's life to flow into us
without limit.
All the things in this world are gifts of God,
presented to us so that we can know God more easily
and make a return of love more readily.
As a result, we appreciate and use all these gifts of God
insofar as they help us develop as loving persons.
But if any of these gifts become the center of our lives,

they displace God and so hinder our growth toward our goal.
In everyday life, then, we must hold ourselves in balance
before all of these created gifts
insofar as we have a choice and are not bound by some obligation.
We should not fix our desires on health or sickness,
wealth or poverty, success or failure, a long life or a short one.
For everything has the potential of calling forth in us
a deeper response to our life in God.
Our only desire and our one choice should be this:
I want and I choose what better leads to God's deepening life in me.

—*Spiritual Exercises of Saint Ignatius Loyola #23*

CHAPTER NINE

One Circle, Many Paths

You will show me the path to life,
abounding joy in your presence.

—Psalm 16:11 (NABRE)

Introduce yourself briefly and tell us why you're here," Fr. José began, "then name your biggest fear about the Camino." The man knew how to get to a point.

After the long bus ride to Azpeitia (the actual town in which the Loyola clan had resided), we checked into simple rooms at a spirituality center sponsored by sisters of the Religious of Jesus and Mary. We enjoyed a warm meal, then gathered in a circle for our orientation meeting. A less skilled facilitator might have started with an easier icebreaker, but Fr. José didn't want us to skim the surface. He wanted us to practice going deep.

Our fears were surprisingly similar. Most of us were worried that we'd packed the wrong things, that our bodies were going to fail us, or that somehow we would fail ourselves by not engaging the experience properly. Betsy—a petite woman with an endearing Southern accent and perfect comic timing—put it best when she confessed to fearing "pilgrim envy." Her husband, Charlie, was the Ignatian volunteer; what if she turned out to be a *remedial* pilgrim, not "holy" enough for the Camino to be effective? When more than one head nodded in recognition, Fr. José encouraged us to resist the temptation to compare ourselves to one another, assuring us that, while each person's experience would be different, God would not be stingy with the divine gifts.

Moving on, he encouraged us to be conscious of the three paths we were about to traverse. The physical path was the obvious one, but we'd be walking it only to deepen our awareness of the other two: the path inward, toward God, and the path outward, toward other people. Learning to walk each one more intentionally would be a true fruit of the Camino.

In order to cultivate awareness of those inner and outer paths, Fr. José explained, we would be spending the first two hours of each walk in prayerful silence, guided by our "pilgrim's book," a spiral-bound treasure trove of readings, prayers, and suggested topics for meditation. As he distributed the books, he recommended that we peruse each day's materials the night before, then draw from them one or two simple points to consider during our morning walk—remembering that less is more. In this way, he gave us a shared experience while allowing us to personalize it.

He cautioned us that, no matter what we decided to pray with, it would be important to pay attention to anything unexpected that bubbled up in the silence. If a particular memory surfaced, for example, we should ask God, "Why now?" and follow that memory wherever it led, for as long as it was meaningful.

As he said this, I remembered something that had popped into my head at a rest stop a few hours earlier as I sipped my first *cortado*—espresso cut with steamed milk, my new favorite beverage. I'd been perhaps six years old when my parents took me to a fancy French restaurant. (An only child at the time, I often got dragged to things beyond my ability to appreciate.) My father ordered an espresso; when it arrived, I totally cracked up at the sight of a grown man drinking from something that looked like it belonged in my dollhouse. My father told that story with delight for the rest of his life. For a moment, right there at orientation, I paused to savor the fond connection with my dad, who had been gone for several years. In the weeks to come, many surprising memories would surface, opening the door to long conversations with God in the silence.

We should be mindful, Fr. José went on, that the landscape itself could be a rich source of reflection, as nature abounds with metaphors for the Divine. Recalling our bus ride, I could easily imagine how this would be true. The topography was so varied; I was glad we'd seen it before setting out across it on foot. Once we got past the ring of industry surrounding Barcelona and the stunning mountains of Montserrat, much of our journey had been through scrubby desert—a possible representation of spiritual dryness. There must have been irrigation, however, because orchards and vineyards dotted the way—reminding me of how we sometimes have to work to stay connected to the Water of

Life. Finally, entering the Basque region, the bus wound its way through a densely forested mountain in the fog. Fr. José explained that the change was a result of our proximity to the sea, and I thought how abundant life can feel when we are awash in an ocean of gratitude.

"All the things in this world are gifts from God," Ignatius wrote in the First Principle and Foundation, "presented to us so that we can know God more easily and make a return of love more readily." I looked forward to walking in deeper awareness of the gifts of creation.

One of those created gifts, Fr. José told us, would serve as the primary metaphor for our pilgrimage: the sunflower—official flower of the Ignatian Camino. Heading steadily east, we would turn our faces to the rising sun, just like those magnificent flowers. Given their abundance on our route, they would serve as frequent reminders to orient our minds and hearts to the light of Christ.

As the meeting drew to a close, Fr. José paused and looked around the circle slowly, letting the anticipation grow, then leaned in and offered one more bit of inspiration. "Pilgrimage can change the world," he said. "I really believe this. Now, let's get ready for tomorrow."

He handed us two important items: our pilgrim's passport, in which we would collect stamps along the Way, and little orange ribbons to identify our suitcases for the daily transport. Before heading to bed, he taught us a customized verse of "The Servant Song," a familiar hymn that became our theme song for the Camino, as we sang it repeatedly each day:

We are pilgrims on a journey;
we're companions on the road.
We are here to help each other
walk the mile and share the load.

Amen!

Mountain, forest, vineyard, orchard, desert: what landscape feels like an apt metaphor for your spiritual life today? What do you need in order to thrive in this terrain?

CHAPTER TEN

In the Room
Where It Happened

For surely I know the plans I have for you, says the LORD,
plans for your welfare and not for harm,
to give you a future with hope.

—Jeremiah 29:11 (NRSVCE)

I awoke in Azpeitia, hardly able to believe I was there. I had first encountered the story of Ignatius's conversion when I was a senior at Saint Joseph's University in the spring of 1987; his autobiography was required reading in my "Jesuit Spirit in Action" class. Thirty-five years later, I was about to be in the room where it happened.

We had caught a glimpse of the dome of the Basilica of St. Ignatius from the bus to Loyola, but the view as you approach it on foot is breathtaking. The Basilica was not our destination, however. Fr. José took us through a side door and there we were—gazing at the outer walls of the Tower House of Loyola, childhood home of Iñigo, as the saint was then known. Entering reverently, we worked our way from room to room.

Pausing at a three-dimensional rendering of Ignatius's head—mounted to indicate his actual height—Fr. José surveyed the group, then said, "Betsy, go stand next to him." We were astonished to discover that the saint was barely taller than our five-foot-one companion!

Finally, we reached the room we'd all been longing to see: the Chapel of the Conversion.

From the ceiling in one corner hangs a fringe of red and gold brocade—a remnant of the room's original bed furnishings. Underneath it sits a gleaming statue of the future saint. He is reclining on a bench, injured leg propped up, eyes gazing heavenward in amazement. One hand holds an open book; the other stretches wide, as though saying, *Take me, Lord.* And indeed, lettering over the altar proclaims, in Euskara (the impenetrable Basque language) as well as Spanish, *"AQUÍ SE*

ENTREGÓ A DIOS IÑIGO DE LOYOLA." Here, Ignatius of Loyola entrusted himself to God.

I could have lingered in that chapel for the rest of the day, but there was much more to see. Fr. José assured us we'd be back for Mass that evening, so off we went to other key sites in the early life of Ignatius. My favorite was the Hermitage of Olatz, a chapel housing a small, painted carving known as Our Lady of the Owls. In both mythology and popular imagination, the owl is a symbol of wisdom because of its large eyes and ability to see in the dark. While this Mary statue looks nothing like an owl (she's a rosy-cheeked figure with normal-sized eyes), the name suggests a place one goes to seek wisdom—as indeed Ignatius had. After he was able to walk again but before he left Loyola, he often took himself to the Hermitage, fifteen minutes away in the forested hills.

I can so imagine Iñigo storming off on a walk, his family assuming he was exercising his bad leg—or possibly just in a bad mood. Once he disappeared into the trees, it would be easy enough to slip into the Hermitage to pray, beseeching Our Lady of the Owls to help him see through the darkness of his searching confusion. Often on our walk, Fr. José would conclude a prayer with "Our Lady of Olatz . . ." to which we would reply, "Pray for us!" We, too, needed wisdom and insight for the journey.

At lunchtime, we headed to a restaurant in a former Augustinian convent and settled ourselves around a long table. I was itching to return to the Chapel before Mass, but I hadn't counted on the length of a Spanish midday meal. Repeatedly, the waitress came to our table and announced the choices for a particular course, which Fr. José would then translate, asking for a show of hands and keeping track of our orders. (This became a regular feature of sit-down meals on the Camino.) After we ate our appetizers, entrees, and dessert, the next time the waitress approached I assumed she was bringing the check. But no—did anyone want coffee? Cappuccino? *Cortado?* Hot tea? (Of the differing Spanish dining customs, I found having coffee *after* dessert to be almost as perplexing as the nine o'clock dinner hour.)

Fortunately, the conversation at my end of the table was as rich as the food. I was seated with Jane, Betsy, and Fr. Nilson Castro, a young Colombian Jesuit who had been on the bus when it pulled up in Barcelona. Fr. Nilson was spending a few months studying spirituality in Manresa; he joined us for our first several days along the Way before picking up the pace and continuing the journey on his own. With four countries and as many continents represented (Jane counting for both Africa and Australia), our intercultural exploration ranged over an intriguing array of topics.

Even the longest lunch ends eventually; when it did, I raced back to our residence to ditch my backpack and change into sandals. (Somehow, my sneakers had given me a blister when I was doing nothing but walking around Azpeitia!) Then finally, *finally*, I was back in the Chapel of the Conversion.

It wasn't a chapel in Ignatius's day; it was the bedroom where he recovered from his injuries at the Battle of Pamplona. During that fateful siege, Iñigo had urged his commander to defend the fortress, even though surrender was the obvious, logical, yet unacceptably humiliating choice.

After one of his legs had been shattered by a French cannonball and the other damaged by shrapnel, Iñigo was bounced home on a litter over fifty mountainous miles. He grew septic; he almost died. His leg healed unattractively, so he insisted they shave down a protruding bone—before the invention of anesthesia. The beatific expression on his golden statue belies the many other faces Ignatius must have made in that room, as he gritted his teeth, threw up, used a bedpan, ached with boredom, and yearned for more stimulating reading than the pious books his sister-in-law, Doña Magdalena, had found for him—until those books began to turn him toward God.

What is now a place of tranquil beauty was predominately a place of pain, as the former swashbuckler suffered from his wounds and lamented his lost future. Even the kernel of insight into the discernment of spirits that he experienced was only that—a kernel, a beginning. He would make many false starts and plunge into near-suicidal despair before fully articulating what we've come to know as Ignatian spirituality.

So, why is that room such a magnet for his followers? I think it's because it brings us closer to the real Ignatius, allowing us to prayerfully imagine the intensity of his months in that room. The chapel is a holy place because beginnings matter: whether we embrace or reject our history, it shapes who we become.

To sit in that room is to sit with Ignatius in agony. Was he remembering those bedridden days when he wrote, "Everything has the potential of calling forth in us a deeper response to our life in God"?

As we imagine Ignatius's suffering, we know it wasn't the end of his story—as it isn't the end of ours. Like him, none of us knows where the path of life will lead. Could the broken swordsman have imagined a statue of himself adorning that very room half a millennium later, with a book rather than a weapon in hand? Could he have dreamed of a basilica bearing his name just beyond the wall, with mahogany doors, multicolored inlaid marble, and a 2,172-pipe organ? The fledgling saint's fantasies of greatness, extravagant though they were, have been exponentially surpassed by reality.

Back in my room that night, in my journal I wrote, *God, please open me to whatever you desire for me on this pilgrimage. Help me let go of my disordered attachments, my superficial wants, my ridiculous convictions about how things "should" be. Let me do all in my power to be fully present wherever you want my attention—the inner or outer journey, the pilgrims or the partner. DEAL WITH ME, sweet Lord!*

Step by step, God drew Ignatius closer. Step by step, God would draw me, as well.

We often talk about Ignatius's "cannonball moment," but in reality, the injury and convalescence that turned him toward God unfolded over a period of months. What painful event from your own past has shaped you? If you gently revisit it, can you sense God with you, never leaving your side while patiently drawing you forward?

CHAPTER ELEVEN

Panning for Gold

Yes, in joy you shall go forth, in peace you shall be brought home;
Mountains and hills shall break out in song before you,
all trees of the field shall clap their hands.

—Isaiah 55:12 (NABRE)

Morning fog shrouded the Basilica of St. Ignatius as we began our fifteen-mile walk to Legazpi. Gathering us at the edge of the compound, Fr. José explained how we would keep track of the route ahead. We should be on the lookout for two things: square plaques with the sunrise logo of the Ignatian Camino, and spray-painted orange arrows. These would be our way signs. If we had any doubt about directions at a fork in the path or street intersection, we should stop and look for one of those symbols.

Of course, we shouldn't need to find our own way. Naturally, we would spread out—we weren't going to walk in one big clump—but even in our prayerful solitude, we should always be able to spot the pilgrims before and behind us. The person in front was never to go so fast that she or he couldn't see the end of the line. (Everything about this ideal was violated early and often, but it was a lovely thought at the beginning.)

We hadn't gone far when we entered a small town and used the public restrooms. I sighed with relief; this had been one of the worries keeping me up at night, but apparently timely morning breaks would be part of our daily routine. (Again, so not true, but a nice way to start.)

Coming to a rail trail paralleling the Urola River, we gathered to begin our two hours of prayerful silence. "Just like Ignatius," Fr. José said, "we walk away from Azpeitia. Like him, we are walking towards something—towards Montserrat, yes, but also towards our growing life within. Not to become a different person, but to change our focus." The group was hushed, awed by the import of what we were about to do. How would the coming weeks change us? We sang our verse of "The Servant Song" and stepped onto the path.

Along a route thick with evergreen trees, we followed the gravel trail through a succession of bridges and tunnels. Above us, forests soared; beneath us, we could spot the winding road on which the bus had traveled two days earlier. Clearings revealed the occasional chapel or grazing donkey, but for the most part we were alone with our thoughts.

I hadn't really been able to picture what it would be like to walk together in silence for such a long time. Would it be awkward, or boring? Would we sneak conversations out of Fr. José's earshot? I needn't have worried. Even walking just a few feet apart, people slipped into a companionable aloneness, finding ample company in our thoughts. When the period of silence was over, we eased back into conversations quietly, as though not wanting to jar one another out of serenity.

At the beginning of the *Exercises'* First Week, Ignatius invites us to reflect on God's love for us and our call to respond. "God, who loves us, gave us life," he wrote. "Our own response of love allows God's life to flow into us without limit." For the next several days, we would be "panning for gold" in prayer: sifting through our memories in response to a series of prompts. On this first walk, the invitation was simple: pondering the goodness of God, who had brought us to this beautiful place at this moment in our lives.

"We walk slowly," our pilgrim's book said, "aware that it is a gift to be able to dedicate time to this encounter with God." A gift, indeed—though we did *not* walk slowly! One of our number, Veronica, had made the Ignatian Camino six years earlier, so she was familiar with the route. Tiny and fit, she set off like a jackrabbit, establishing a pace that would last throughout the month. Though I'd always identified as a fast walker, I was surprised to find myself at the back of the pack immediately.

Later, I learned that Veronica was in a great deal of pain at the start of the Camino. Originally from Malaysia, she'd been living in Melbourne, Australia, when her younger (and only) sister died after a swift battle with stage-four cancer. Angeline's death was recent, and a tremendous blow. The first time Veronica had walked the Camino, her sister had shared the journey vicariously, absorbing all her stories. Angeline's absence this time left Veronica feeling terribly lonely—and her sciatica didn't help. While pain and sorrow might grind some of us to a halt, Veronica discovered that moving swiftly brought her a modicum of emotional distraction and even physical relief. We really never know what others are carrying.

The pattern established that first day continued throughout the Camino. Fr. José would tell the front walker where to stop—either at a particular time or landmark—in order to give the back of our human Slinky time to catch up before starting out again. (Lamentably, often this meant that the energetic people in front got rest breaks, while the exhausted ones in back did not. I'd reach a designated stopping point and touch base with Porter, only to hear Fr. José announce, "Okay, pilgrims, let's go!") The sixty-three-year-old priest—only slightly younger than the median age of his charges—worked the line like a coach, ambling back and forth to check on everyone. In this fashion, he joked, he actually walked many more miles than the rest of us. While Fr. Nilson was there, he intentionally brought up the rear to keep an eye on the stragglers; consequently, I often enjoyed his company.

On that first day's walk, I was distracted from prayer by the pace, but also by the fact that the patch of moleskin I'd slapped over my Loyola blister did not seem to be doing its job. The outside of my left heel was complaining with every step. I decided to resort to an old-fashioned Catholic practice: offering it up.

We were supposed to be praying for a felt sense of God's love for us, so I decided to offer my physical misery for those who do not experience an intimate awareness of God's love. I let my mind wander among people I knew, holding them in the light, interceding for them, and asking how I might be a better instrument of God's love in their regard. Allowing my pain to connect me to others became one of the most moving parts of the Camino for me.

Recalling that Fr. José had invited us to focus on the surrounding beauty, I began pondering the many tunnels we were walking through. Who had done this hard work—first to build a railway, then to convert it to a trail—enabling me to stride through the mountain passes instead of summiting or going around? I decided to pray for those who do hard jobs that make life easier for others, and quickly shifted from the general to the particular: who did I know personally who had done hard things that made life easier for me?

I thought about my Irish ancestors, driven by the potato famine to start over in a foreign country so their descendants could prosper. I remembered my maternal grandfather, who had put three daughters through college and lived carefully within his means; though he died of cardiac arrest in his fifties, I am one of the beneficiaries of both his wise investments and his commitment to the education of women. I thought of my parents, both teachers, who never had a lot of money but who insisted I limit my working hours in college so I could focus on my studies and extracurricular activities: acting, writing, and campus ministry, all of which have served me well. Reaching the present day, I gave thanks for Porter, who often dives into jobs I consider too difficult (or yucky) to tackle myself.

Three miles shy of our destination, we paused at an outdoor café in Urretxu to eat the lunches the sisters at the retreat house in Azpeitia had made for us. By mid-afternoon, we'd arrived in a little town called Legazpi and checked into the Hotel Mauleon. After showering and doing my "sink laundry," I stretched with Betsy on the front porch before enjoying a beer with several pilgrims on the patio of the hotel bar. Eventually, I shifted to my own table so I could keep an ear on their friendly chatter while writing a brief account of our day and selecting accompanying photos to send to IVC. (Though beers at the bar turned out to be a rare treat, curating photos remained a daily ritual.)

Afterward, Porter and I explored the town a bit, visiting the local church and buying lunch for the next day at a small grocery store. After a late dinner in the hotel dining room, one task remained, but it was a doozie: figuring out what to do about my blister.

Many people had weighed in on the question, offering both opinions and supplies, but my gut said I should seek help from Jane and Tony. They welcomed me into their room, and Jane pulled out assorted first aid supplies while I took off my sock. My blister had blown up like a grape. "Well now, I don't think I've ever seen one that large," the veteran hiker exclaimed. (*That can't be good*, I thought.) Undeterred, Jane demonstrated what I should do: send a needle and thread through the base of the blister, press out the fluid, leave the thread in place to serve as a wick, cover the whole thing with the pad of a Band-Aid, and secure it with a paper tape called Micropore. Since I had almost none of those supplies, she loaded me up and sent me back to my room, where Porter and I engaged in the first session of what would come to be known as "blister camp."

What a day it had been! Reading my pilgrim's book in bed, I remembered that one of Fr. José's suggested Scriptures for the day had been a passage from Isaiah 55 (10–11, NABRE):

> Yet just as from the heavens
> the rain and snow come down
> And do not return there
> till they have watered the earth,
> making it fertile and fruitful,
> Giving seed to the one who sows
> and bread to the one who eats,
> So shall my word be
> that goes forth from my mouth;
> It shall not return to me empty,
> but shall do what pleases me,
> achieving the end for which I sent it.

I have loved that passage for decades; often it shows up when I'm struggling to believe that the work I'm doing in the moment will yield good fruit in the end. Isaiah reminds me that *God's* work unfolds over time—sometimes a lot of time.

This Camino would be fruitful, I told myself. I didn't need to know how—yet.

When have you experienced God's work unfolding over time? Is there something you are still waiting to see come to fruition? If so, hold that in mind as you pray Isaiah's words above.

CHAPTER TWELVE
Mothering

As a mother comforts her child,
so I will comfort you.

—Isaiah 66:13 (NRSVCE)

We left Legazpi before sunrise. The intensity of the first hike had caught me by surprise, yet apparently that had been an "easy" walk. *This* day was going to be challenging, the ordinarily unflappable Fr. José warned us. We were ascending into the Aizkorri mountain range to visit the Shrine of Our Lady of Arantzazu, where Ignatius had spent a night in prayer five hundred years earlier. Fr. José encouraged us to remember that the effort would be worth it because, like Ignatius, we were going to visit the Blessed Mother.

I pondered this idea with more than a touch of skepticism as we propelled ourselves prayerfully through the early-morning streets. (Prayerful propelling feels as oxymoronic as it sounds, though eventually I got the knack of it.) Much as I desired to walk in the footsteps of Ignatius, climbing a mountain to visit a statue I'd never heard of was not exactly part of my spirituality.

Suddenly, this thought overwhelmed me: *If I knew I was going to see my own mother*—gone fifteen years at that point—*what would I not be willing to do to get there?* Swift tears blurred my vision. I will never stop missing my mom, but usually the ache lies dormant. That day, however, physical stress and emotional rawness brought my longing to the surface. *What would I not give to feel her near me again?*

Quiet footsteps recalled me to the present moment, and I realized that the person walking next to me was Jane. I had been moved by her tender care not twelve hours earlier, when she taught me how to mend my dramatic blister, and here she was at the very moment I was missing my mother so fiercely. Most of the group referred to her as Aussie Jane (to distinguish her from Canada Jane, whose backpack sported a mapleleaf bandana in honor of her dual citizenship with our neighbor to the north), but from that moment on, she was Mama Jane to me—and her mothering continued throughout the day.

Entering the Aizkorri-Aratz Natural Park, we ascended alarmingly steep terrain over treacherous rocks for three hours (climbing the equivalent of sixty-eight floors, my iPhone estimates). The pace, altitude, and unrelenting grade left me shaking and winded. Pausing to catch my breath caused my head to pound. I didn't know how I could possibly keep going, yet what was the alternative? There was no helicopter coming to pluck me off the mountain.

Once again, Mama Jane appeared at my shoulder—this time on purpose. "Give me your pack," she commanded. Jane is ten years older and several inches shorter than I am, so at first, I resisted; *absolutely not!* But she was as firm as my own mother would have been. "Right now, every ounce makes a difference. I'm used to carrying far more weight than this. Give it to me!" I agreed to let her take my pack for ten minutes or until we caught up with the group. The next time she asked, I handed it over more graciously. Later, I spotted my pack on Charlie's shoulder, and was too exhausted to be anything but grateful.

In addition to her physical help, Mama Jane knew how to support my flagging spirits. "I'm going to 'Good King Wenceslas' you for a while" she announced on flatter terrain. Immediately, I recalled—in Bing Crosby's rich baritone—the plot of the old Christmas carol. King Wenceslas and his servant walked out on a harsh winter night to bring supper to a poor man. Buffeted by any icy wind, the king made a surprising invitation: "Mark my footsteps, my good page; tread thou in them boldly. Thy shalt find the winter's rage freeze thy blood less coldly." The servant complied: "In his master's steps he trod, where the snow lay dinted; heat was in the very sod which the saint had printed." Jane got in front of me and walked purposefully at a pace she thought I could manage. Resolutely, I placed my feet where her saintly hiking boots had trod; this warmed my heart and enabled me to press on.

Later that afternoon, we had to make our way down the other side of the mountain. Fog had rendered the rocks wet with mud; almost everyone fell at least once, though no one suffered injuries to anything but their dignity. With the worst of the descent behind us, Jane changed tactics, telling me stories to get my mind off my feet. Eventually, I felt well enough to check on other pilgrims, posing conversation-opening questions to help pass the miles. Like all good mothering, Mama Jane's ministrations had not rendered me dependent, but empowered me to offer my own form of care.

Finally, we arrived at the place Ignatius had set out to visit upon leaving Loyola: the Sanctuary of Arantzazu. When he arrived, the shrine had been a site of devotion for over fifty years, ever since—the legend goes—a shepherd following the sound of a cowbell discovered a small statue of the Blessed Mother caught in a thorn bush. (In Euskara, Arantza-zu means "You—among the thorns?") Shortly after the shepherd's discovery, a drought ended and a civil conflict subsided. With gratitude for what was perceived as Mary's intervention, Franciscan friars built a chapel at the site, which immediately became a place of pilgrimage.

Three times in the last five hundred years, fire has destroyed the Shrine while leaving the statue undamaged. The present Basilica is a massive stone and iron structure that looks like part of the mountain itself. High in the front of the church sits Our Lady of the Thorns— barely bigger than the cowbell that still accompanies her. A friar led us up back stairs (ugh, more climbing!) to the top level, where he pushed a button to make the statue revolve toward us so we could see her face more clearly.

Honestly, there is nothing remarkable about that statue. It is not grand, or even particularly pretty. The Shrine derives its powerful sense of holiness from the generations of pilgrims who have ascended the mountain to pray there, entrusting their cares to Mary's intercession. As we celebrated Mass, we lifted up people we knew who were caught in life's thorny dilemmas. It was the wedding day of my friend Jillian's daughter, so I prayed that the Blessed Mother would protect Allison and Matt from the thorns of conflict.

That night, we stayed in the Goiko Benta Hostel, a charming inn that predated Ignatius's visit. "Does that mean he slept here?" I asked Fr. José. "Well," he said, laughing, "he was keeping an all-night vigil, so probably not . . . But we can say Ignatius's *mule* slept here!"

What to make of this hard, strange, and memorable day? At age fifty-seven, far from home and farther from my comfort zone, I felt inept as a child and ashamed of my ineptitude. Yet what lingers is my sense of being surrounded by a trinity of mothers—Jesus's mother, my own, and one I'd just met. Together, they sustained me in ways both spiritual and practical.

In the shadow of Our Lady of the Thorns, I fell into an untroubled sleep.

Who has mothered you—literally, metaphorically, or spiritually? In prayer, imagine your mother figures on earth and in heaven gathered around you, loving you, interceding for you, and desiring nothing but your good. What arises in you as you ponder that image?

CHAPTER THIRTEEN
The Mercies

The steadfast love of the LORD never ceases,
his mercies never come to an end;
they are new every morning.

—Lamentations 3:22–23 (NRSVCE)

I t was still pitch dark when my alarm went off the next morning. I swung my feet to the floor and chugged the contents of my twenty-four-ounce water bottle, to which I'd added a hydration tablet the night before. Next, I limped to the bathroom, where I'd staged what I needed to make a small but potent cup of instant. My barista duties complete, I slipped out of our room and took my coffee and pilgrim's book to a sofa in the common area to pray. With minor variations—like when there was real coffee available somewhere, or nowhere to slip but back into bed—this would be how I started every day. Some people (including Porter) arose as late as possible to get the maximum rest, but what I most required was a good ninety minutes to ready myself physically, spiritually, and emotionally for whatever lay ahead.

We left Arantzazu, and the path began to ascend again. At first, I was afraid to look up. My experience the previous day had taught me to keep my eyes on my feet, as checking to see how far I had to go yielded only despair. Fortunately, this day's terrain would be varied enough for me to gauge the distance from one breather to the next. Whenever I could unglue my eyes from the path, I felt a rush of gratitude.

Raising my eyes raised my spirits, as I savored the world around me. I'd turn a bend or summit a hill and gasp at the landscape: mountaintops draped in clouds; sunlight piercing foggy forests; lush green fields sprinkled with boulders. A solitary tree loomed over a precipice, its root ball seemingly suspended in mid-air. ("I always check to make sure this is still here," Fr. José said. "It gives me hope!") Grazing animals welcomed us with their cheerful bells; at one point I delighted in the sight—and sound—of a comically noisy flock of sheep commuting in the opposite direction.

Looking up also enabled me to spot the trail markers more effectively—which was good, because I'd lost sight of the pilgrims ahead of me. Pivoting at a marker for a hairpin uphill turn, I remembered that I had passed Kathy maybe fifty yards back. Now, Kathy is a no-nonsense mother of six and a veteran of the *Camino de Santiago*; I suspect she would have had no trouble spotting the orange arrow. Still, I slowed my steps a bit, waiting to be sure she'd caught it. As she turned, Kathy met my eyes, smiled, and nodded. I felt a rush of gladness to be a contributing member for a change.

We continued to climb and descend for three more days before emerging from the mountains, but we never repeated the unrelenting ascent we'd experienced on the way to Arantzazu; instead, the ups and downs were interspersed with brief level stretches. As Fr. José had predicted, nature was yielding insight. Even in the hardest life—or the hardest stretch of a regular life—the "terrain" is not uniformly impossible. Sweet moments of solace abound, if we are willing to appreciate those moments on their own terms.

I began calling level stretches *the mercies,* as in "Lord, have mercy!" followed by "Oh good, here comes another mercy." Having served as a campus minister at Gwynedd Mercy University for fifteen years, I spent some time recalling the many Sisters and other women and men of Mercy I'd been privileged to know. As I prayed for each in turn, the memories took my mind off the miles.

We were walking alongside a gently sloping ravine with a creek at the bottom when Fr. José stopped us for lunch. Many of the pilgrims scrambled down the hill and spread out, finding fallen tree trunks to serve as picnic benches, but I couldn't face the return climb. I found a spot on the side of the road and removed my boots and socks, arranging them so I could rest my bare feet in the sun. Charlie joined me, shaking his head about what could possibly be motivating people to venture down the embankment into the buggy unknown, just to eat their lunch. I'd been admiring Charlie's sense of humor in group conversations and welcomed the opportunity to get to know him a little better. In addition to his IVC service with Meals on Wheels, he was enjoying a post-retirement adventure as a "Boston by Foot" tour guide. Since I had lived in the North End of Boston through grad school, we immediately began comparing favorite Beantown haunts. While we talked, we enjoyed the sandwiches from our lunch packs while speculating what they might contain, as the rolls were filled with something tasty yet unidentifiable. (Fr. José later informed us that they were tuna omelet sandwiches—apparently a common menu item in Spain. He was surprised to learn that Americans put neither tuna in their omelets nor omelets in their sandwiches.)

Restored by the pause, we pressed on. A long level stretch followed. I fell into step with Porter and Jim, but when talk turned to American football, I lengthened my stride and caught up with some of the women. We stopped at the designated location, where I had the new experience of sitting in the shade waiting for others to catch up. Eventually, Porter appeared—bent like a question mark and leaning on Fr. José's walking stick. Oh, no! Something wonky had happened with his back. It was slow going to our next resting place, the *Casa de Oración* (House of Prayer) in Eguino.

A divine wink lifted my spirits, however, when I discovered that the retreat center was run by . . . wait for it . . . Sisters of Mercy! Clearly, I had my word for the day.

At the House of Prayer, we each got a modest room with a twin bed and a tiny bathroom; it was our most spartan accommodation yet. And yet—hallelujah—there was a washing machine downstairs! Fr. José pushed a cart through the hallways, crying, "Laundry, Laundry!" There were no dryers, so we hung everything on a line in the courtyard.

After dinner, I got Porter settled in with Aleve and a CBD-oil massage, then took some time to settle myself, unnerved by this new development. What if he was no better in the morning? What if his back was badly injured? (Whoops—those what-ifs again!) Fortunately,

I recalled one of my favorite Jan Richardson blessings, "For Those Who Have Far to Travel," which we'd used in our Commissioning not two weeks earlier. It includes this marvelous line:

> Call it
> one of the mercies
> of the road:
> that we see it
> only by stages
> as it opens
> before us,
> as it comes into
> our keeping,
> step by
> single step.

Wasn't that the truth! Gratified as I had been whenever I spotted a "mercy" on the path earlier that day, I did not need to know everything that was coming. Sometimes—on the Way as in life—it was a mercy *not* to know. I just needed to be present to what was before me: the beauty, the challenge, and the occasional solace, which was mercy enough.

Fearing it might rain overnight but uncertain if the door was alarmed, someone asked Fr. José if we could go out at bedtime to bring the wash inside.

"Maybe," the priest deadpanned. "But if you wake these sisters, *I will kill you.*"

Even mercy has its limits.

That day on the Camino, my idea of "mercy" was physical: getting a break from the punishing terrain. That's akin to mercy's legal connotation: receiving clemency instead of punishment. In each case, the appropriate response is gratitude—yet both pale in comparison to the mercy of God. When have you been on the receiving end of mercy? To whom might you be called to extend it?

CHAPTER FOURTEEN
Solidarities

Bear one another's burdens, and in this way you will fulfill
the law of Christ.

—Galatians 6:2 (NRSVCE)

A good night's sleep rendered Porter upright again, though he did turn into "question mark man" several more times over the course of the next few weeks, as weariness overtook his spine. Whenever that happened, I made sure to walk nearby—not so close as to appear to be hovering, but close enough that he didn't feel alone. (He just told me he has no recollection of my doing that. I'm going to go ahead and assume it helped him anyway.)

As for me, though the beneficiaries kept changing, my commitment to "offering up" the aches and pains of the journey continued. Beginning the silent part of each day's walk, I would notice what I was experiencing, then let my feelings serve as a doorway to prayer.

Faced with yet another long hike, for example, I prayed for people who have to get up and do difficult things every day, such as parents of young children and those caring for dying loved ones. Falling behind the pack, I prayed for older folks who have trouble walking and for students who can't keep up with their peers. Spotting a barking dog in a sad enclosure, I lifted up people who are imprisoned, whether behind bars or in the snares of addiction. Grateful for the support of my traveling companions, I asked God's blessing on all whose lives are marked by loneliness. Each day, I tried to walk in solidarity with people who were hurting, letting my pain connect me to the pain of others.

Sifting through my memories, I put names and faces on those intercessions, but I also tried to be mindful of the multitude of suffering souls whose faces I would never see. During a group reflection one evening, I discovered that many of us had the same population in mind as we walked: migrants and refugees.

As of this writing, the United Nations High Commissioner for Refugees (UNHCR) estimates that there are over one hundred million forcibly displaced individuals worldwide. The longer and hotter a day's journey was, the more those people weighed on our hearts. There we were, with our weight-distributing backpacks, insulated water bottles, collapsible hiking poles, moisture-wicking socks, and multiple pairs of shoes. Our route was mapped, our rooms reserved, our luggage transported, and our meals assured—inconceivable luxuries to the men, women, and children trekking across continents in search of safe haven.

"We're only doing this for thirty days," I lamented. "And we volunteered for it."

Fr. José shook his head as he laughed. "Volunteered for it? You *paid* for this!"

Here's what I realized: the value of placing myself in solidarity with others depends on what I do with the feelings that arise. Pope St. John Paul II articulated that challenge in his encyclical "On Social Concern" when he wrote, "[Solidarity] is not a feeling of vague compassion or shallow distress at the misfortunes of so many people, both near and far. On the contrary, it is a firm and persevering determination to commit oneself to the common good."

Strengthening that "firm and persevering determination" is a fruit of the Camino that I am trying to cultivate. Allowing my discomfort to connect me to people in pain grooved one of the interior paths Fr. José had talked about—the one that led outward, toward others. But the end of that path needed to be action, not just empathy or even prayer, as we are called to be God's hands on this earth. "God has an image of a perfect world," Fr. José said more than once, "But it is not perfect. So, what is my part? What am I called to do?" His questions underscored our days.

I was moved by one example of solidarity-in-action when Louise—who celebrated her sixty-eighth birthday on the Camino—explained why she has purple hair. She volunteers in a juvenile detention center, and when a person her age walks in the door, she said, the kids think "old lady" and check out. But an old lady with purple tresses—now, that elicits a different reaction. Cool Grandma is a walking icebreaker, her hair an instant conversation starter—and more of a commitment than some hip outfit she could don and doff at will. Without a word, Louise conveyed, "I'm willing to look like this in my world so I can more easily enter yours." She empathized with those incarcerated kids, she prayed for them, and—with the help of a bottle of hair dye—she aligned herself with them.

Solidarity is a stance, not a feeling. How do we stand with people in pain—those we know, and those we only know about? Along the way, I did what I could, not just praying for people, but sending off brief emails at night to tell them they'd been on my mind. Since returning home, I've tried to let those prayers lead to practical assistance whenever possible, both within my circle of care and beyond it. A donation to Jesuit Refugee Services hits my credit card every month now, and when it does, I am transported back to our conversations along the Way. It's a start—but only a start.

As pilgrims on the journey of life, we are called to keep asking the question: *Who cries out for my prayers, words, dollars, or actions today?* Fr. José said that pilgrimage can change the world. Imagine a world filled with pilgrims committed to asking—and answering—that question. Who knows what changes we might effect?

When I talk about offering it up, I'm not suggesting that you "just remember everyone who has it worse," as though adding guilt to your pain will somehow make it easier to bear. I simply mean that hearts and minds are expansive; we are capable of great compassion even under duress. Suffering can isolate us, but it can also connect us to the great web of humanity. Who does your pain connect you to? Who cries out for your compassion today?

CHAPTER FIFTEEN
Shelter

You are my shelter; you guard me from distress;
with joyful shouts of deliverance you surround me.

—Psalm 32:7 (NABRE)

In Santa Cruz de Campezo, we stayed at our first pilgrims' shelter. I'd been anxious, not knowing what to expect, but the *Aterpea* was a marvel: a brand-new facility constructed especially for the Ignatian Camino. The rooms were bright, cheery, and thoughtfully designed; each bunk bed had clothes hooks, interior shelves, power outlets—even reading lights. Most exciting for me was the coffee machine in the dining room; instead of making instant sludge in the morning, I could get a *cortado* for just one euro!

Still, I'd slept badly the night before, and that day's hike had been rough. Only eleven miles, but it had rained for a while, and the terrain was like something out of *The Lord of the Rings*—craggy and mucky, with a steep ninety minutes of climbing. I'd been able to carry my own backpack the whole way, though, in part because "Lighten up!" had taken on a literal meaning. (When we sat to catch our breath, for example, I'd eaten the apple in my lunch pack because it was heavier than the sandwich.) I do remember one graced moment, when Fr. José halted us in a forest clearing for a few minutes of prayer, inviting us to breathe in the evergreen fragrance and offer thanks for the beauty all around us. Unfortunately, it was not enough to elevate my mood for long.

By the time we arrived at the *Aterpea,* my boots were caked in mud, my bright blue rain poncho was soaked, and I was cranky. Fr. José gave us our electronic keys and directed us to the bunk rooms—one for the women, another for the men. This created a hurdle for the couples, who'd been accustomed to having access to one another's luggage. A scramble ensued: Who had the Aleve? The Band-Aids? The phone charger?

Though I'd been in their company almost every waking hour for six days, sharing a room with nine women was going to be a new level of togetherness. I claimed a bottom bunk near a window with floor space for my ridiculous suitcase, navigated the shower and sink-laundry queues, strung my clothesline from the upper bunk, dealt with my blister, set an alarm for thirty minutes, and fell sound asleep.

Surprisingly restored by my catnap, I found Porter and we walked the few blocks to the center of town to buy lunch for the next day. In addition to our usual bread and cheese, we snagged a dark chocolate bar and a bag of nuts—serious energy for the journey! The town square featured a fountain surrounded by tables and chairs where we spotted some of our fellow pilgrims relaxing, enjoying snacks from the grocery and beverages from a nearby tavern. We joined them in the midst of a lively discussion about the dangers of unfettered capitalism—hardly your typical happy-hour chatter. How heartening it was to explore ideas with like-minded souls, knowing that the conversation could continue over the next few weeks.

After a family-style dinner in a restaurant—a big salad and the first of many Spanish omelets—we returned to the pilgrims' shelter, where I slept better in a roomful of women than I had in my own private cell the night before. I woke early, dressed quietly in the dark, and tiptoed downstairs. Over not one but two *cortados,* I crafted a reflection for IVC to send out to those who were following our travels. (One "comfort item" I never regretted packing was a lightweight wireless keyboard that enabled me to type on my phone using all ten fingers instead of my clumsy thumbs.) Gradually, the dining room filled up, and breakfast fruit and pastry appeared. Someone wandered away from a toaster oven and set off the smoke alarm. A new day had begun.

Along the Camino, our accommodations varied widely. There were queen beds in "two-star" hotels, twin beds in hostels, bunk beds in pilgrims' shelters, and—once—air mattresses on the floor of a day-care center. Though I was always grateful for the nicer places, anxiety about the pilgrims' shelters dissipated after my good experience at the *Aterpea.*

I realized that privacy is as much mental as physical; in the bunk rooms, each woman granted the others the illusion of solitude that allowed us to retreat inside our own minds. Alone with our thoughts, we read, wrote, prayed, and slept. Grateful for the camaraderie of the day, at night we rested in the shelter of one another.

———————————

Let your mind wander among various places where you have found shelter over the years. Which have felt like gifts from God? Savor the particulars of hospitality you've received, and rest in gratitude.

CHAPTER SIXTEEN
It's in There

*The word is very near to you; it is in your mouth
and in your heart for you to observe.*

—Deuteronomy 30:14 (NRSVCE)

I know we're supposed to be praying during the first two hours of every walk. Does repeatedly taking the name of the Lord in vain count?"

I cracked this joke at the end of a particularly pressured segment of hiking, but I wasn't actually swearing my way across Spain. The only truth in that snarky remark was the word "repeatedly." When the pace or terrain overwhelmed my ability to pray deeply (by which I mean conversationally, meditatively, or imaginatively), I took comfort in repeating words and phrases lodged in my memory.

It began during that long ascent to Arantzazu. Knowing that we were going to "visit" the Blessed Mother, I was thrown back to one of my mom's favorite prayers, the *Memorare:*

Remember, O most gracious Virgin Mary,
that never was it known
that anyone who fled to your protection,
implored your help,
or sought your intercession,
was left unaided.
Inspired by this confidence
I fly unto you,
O Virgin of virgins, my Mother.
To you do I come,
before you I stand,
sinful and sorrowful.
O Mother of the Word Incarnate,
despise not my petitions,
but in your mercy hear and answer me.

I recalled my mother confessing that she had prayed a *Memorare* on her knees for me every night during the college summer I'd spent down the shore. (My cousin Susan and I were working at a Christian gift shop in the one dry town on the South Jersey coast, but it was my first time living away from home, and moms worry.) I hadn't thought of that prayer in years, but now it came back to me whole. As I grew more exhausted by the climb, I resorted to repeating the last sentence like a mantra, in cadence with my steps: *O Mother of the Word Incarnate, despise not my petitions, but in your mercy hear and answer me.*

Gradually, other words emerged from the deep. Once upon a time I'd memorized a few prayers in Spanish, so I was able to pass a satisfying hour trying to drag those beloved lines out of the mental vault. Later, I challenged myself to piece together all four verses of Tagore's "Friends Whom I Knew Not," which I'd quoted extensively in my book *Finding God Abiding*. In both cases, something about the combination of meaningful words and mental exercise sustained me for quite a while.

Various Scripture passages joined the parade of words in my head. Walking through the mountains, I recalled Psalm 121:1 (NRSVCE), "I lift up my eyes to the hills—from where will my help come?" Remembering that I'd prayed Psalm 121 in the mountains of Vermont on the day I learned that my friend Ron's son Oliver had died, I paused to hold Ron in the light. On another day, I clung to St. Peter's incredulous exclamation after Jesus asked if he wanted to jump ship like other faint-hearted followers: "Lord, to whom shall we go? You have the words of everlasting life." Mile after mile, the rhythmic "Lord, to whom shall we go?" reminded me that there was nowhere I'd rather be.

Certain hymns also provided prayerful refuge. (The world seems divided between people who always have a tune in their head and those who do not; I'm firmly among the former.) Gospel songs such as "Guide My Feet" and "We've Come This Far by Faith" encouraged me to press on. The sight of a little dead bird evoked "His Eye is on the Sparrow," assuring me that I was not alone.

Even though such repetitive prayer isn't ordinarily my style, I'm grateful to have had access to such richness under duress. I credit three inspirations. First applause goes to my mother, who could recite long poems decades after learning them; she often lamented the disappearance of memorization as an educational strategy. Next there are the Liturgy of the Hours and daily Mass; decades of repetition have grooved the words of Scripture into my brain. Finally, there's music ministry; though choir members usually grow sick of certain hymns just when the congregation comes to love them, we do absorb a great deal of theology set to music.

In the age of smartphones, the ability to "look anything up" is both a gift and a curse. Though vast amounts of information are there at our fingertips, the convenience discourages committing things to memory. But even if I'd had cell service in the Cantabrian mountains, what would I have done—pulled out my phone and said, "Hey Siri: What's a good prayer, poem, Scripture, or song for when you've climbed higher than you would have thought possible but still have an impossible distance to go?" (Okay, I just tried it, and got a link to "30 Prayers to Give You Peace of Mind When You Need It Most," but there's no way I could have flipped through them without dropping my phone or dropping out of the pack!)

Back in the late 80s, a series of Prego spaghetti sauce commercials featured the slogan "It's in there!" (All the ingredients a home cook could want, right in one convenient jar.) *Prego* is Italian for "You're welcome," so perhaps that's God's response as I offer thanks for all the heartening words that dwell in my memory banks and offer themselves as needed. *"Prego!"*

What's hanging out in your memory banks? Lines of poetry, Scripture passages, bits of hymns, favorite quotes, pop song lyrics, movie lines? Which of these can you summon in times of trouble? If you feel like you don't have much in reserve, consider starting a "commonplace book" to capture what inspires you.

CHAPTER SEVENTEEN

Indifference

I know indeed how to live in humble circumstances;
I know also how to live with abundance.
In every circumstance and in all things I have learned the
secret of being well fed and of going hungry,
of living in abundance and of being in need.
I have the strength for everything through him who empowers me.

—Philippians 4:12–13 (NABRE)

Leaving Santa Cruz de Campezo, I devoted the whole morning's walk to the First Principle and Foundation of the *Spiritual Exercises*, praying with its most challenging passage: the one on Ignatian indifference. "We should not fix our desires on health or sickness, wealth or poverty, success or failure, a long life or a short one. For everything has the potential of calling forth in us a deeper response to our life in God."

Rummaging prayerfully, I considered each pair of opposites in turn, wondering which to prefer.

Health or Sickness? Who wouldn't rather be healthy? One week into the Camino, I was grateful not to have had any muscle strains, morning migraines, or digestive distress—three of my many "what-ifs" before the trip. Yet I was even more grateful for the way my angry blister and shaky legs had opened the door to intimacy with Mama Jane. Would we have befriended each other so early if I hadn't needed her help? Perhaps that meant I needed to be grateful for my infirmities as well.

Good health, of course, is a tenuous thing; I knew a Camino injury was no more than a poorly placed hiking boot away. Already, one of our number had been felled by a stomach bug. Was it contagious? While I hoped I would remain well, I tried to heed Ignatius's instruction not to fix my desire on good health. *God, help me be accepting of whatever comes,* I prayed.

Wealth or Poverty? That was another tough one. Thinking of the insecurity that burdens the lives of people in poverty, I knew I'd take wealth in a heartbeat, given the choice. And yet, Ignatius hadn't *posed* a choice; he simply said we should not fix our desires on either extreme. It is hard to imagine fixing our desires on poverty, yet the newly converted Ignatius had done precisely that, pursuing poverty to the detriment of his physical health. For the rest of us, I suspect, the more tempting danger is pursuing wealth to the detriment of our spiritual health: hoarding what we have, ever longing for more. The challenge, I mused, would be to stay honest about my relationship with money and material goods, which I want to be marked by gratitude and generosity. *Never take security for granted,* I told myself as I walked, *but regard it as an instrument for doing good in the world. Strive for simplicity. Give wholeheartedly.*

Success or Failure? This was more familiar territory. In my wallet, I keep a slip of fortune cookie wisdom: "We learn little from success, but much from failure." Believing that failure has educative value, however, does not remove the sting of a botched endeavor. As I walked, I lingered with memories of times I had let people down, personally and professionally. In particular, I pondered my first marriage—the red flags I'd ignored, the poor choices I'd made, and the pain I'd caused during our six-year union.

The note in my pilgrim's book said that we should be "holding our whole life up to God." Rather than suppressing or rationalizing those painful memories away, I tried to hold them gently. *Yesterday's failures are part of my story,* I thought, *part of what makes me a compassionate listener to other people's stories today. For this, I can be grateful.*

Long Life or Short One? Ah, an easy one at last. I decided I was okay with either (though arguably, at fifty-seven, a short life was no longer an option). In my journal that night, I wrote, *I'd rather not have a too-long life with a lot of pain at the end or go so early that my loved ones are devastated, but You take me when You want me, Lord!*

Each of Ignatius's pairs of opposites was grounded in experience. As a young, swashbuckling courtier, he had pursued the more "worldly" options vigorously. In the early years after his conversion, he reversed course: intentionally neglecting his health, begging for alms, running afoul of the Spanish Inquisition, and even dreaming of martyrdom.

Having chased after every extreme before coming to balance, Ignatius knew what he was talking about when he said that no decision should be made under the influence of an inordinate attachment. The key that helps me unlock this meditation is the word "fix." When Ignatius warns against *fixing* our desires, I picture a science museum display of butterflies: each gorgeous creature permanently fastened to a board. When we fix our desire on something, we close ourselves off to other possibilities—like the graced assistance we may receive during illness, or the lessons we can learn through failure. Ignatius wanted us to pay attention to our desires as the living things they are, allowing them to float freely as a way of discerning *God's* desires for us.

On the far side of the Camino, I'm still practicing Pilates, balancing my checkbook, employing a skilled editor, and watching my cholesterol—things that support my health, wealth, success, and longevity. But I try to keep the outcomes in perspective, trusting with Ignatius that *everything* has the potential of calling forth a deeper response to my life in God.

Near the end of the hike from Santa Cruz to Laguardia, the once-distant peak of the *León Dormido* (a mountain shaped like a sleeping lion, which we'd been approaching for days), appeared within reach. Emerging from the forest onto a gently sloping path, we gasped in wonder as we beheld the Rioja valley, spread out like a patchwork comforter as far as the eye could see. All that remained was to walk out of the mountains.

As we started down the path, loose gravel caused my feet to shoot out from under me and I landed hard on my hip and elbow. Though I wasn't injured, both Mama Jane and Fr. Nilson stayed by my side for the next few miles. This turned out to be a great blessing, as it paved the way for one of the most memorable conversations of our journey.

A few days earlier, the group had celebrated Jane and Tony's thirty-eighth anniversary with a bottle of champagne in Azpeitia. Knowing that part of his ministry would be preparing couples for matrimony, Fr. Nilson now asked Jane what she saw as the secret to a successful marriage. Jane answered swiftly with a three-point plan. (Clearly, she had given this some thought.) Touched by her words, I asked her to repeat them, then recorded them in my journal that night:

1) Work on it every day.
2) Always desire the best for your partner.
3) Don't go out for the first coffee.

Numbers one and two are self-explanatory, but I pressed her on the third. (What's wrong with the first coffee? I love it when Porter fetches early coffee for me!) It wasn't about the caffeine, though. When you hit a rocky patch in your relationship, Jane explained, don't be the first to seek consolation elsewhere (in another person, job, cause, etc.). If neither of you "goes out for the first coffee," you are more likely to stay and work it out together.

Jane's wisdom was worth pondering. How do hard times affect us? The First Principle and Foundation says that everything has the potential to "call forth a deepening of our life in God," but it is only *potential*. Challenges also can cause us to start formulating an exit strategy, even if subconsciously. In faith and in relationships, love requires mindfulness.

I was grateful for the humble curiosity that had led Fr. Nilson to pose his question. What a good priest he must be!

As we approached Laguardia, the landscape itself presented an opportunity to practice Ignatian indifference. "You're going to miss the mountains," Fr. José said, chuckling. Hard as that was to believe, I felt a surprising pang of nostalgia for the terrain of the first few days. In the weeks to come, our steps would take us through vineyards and deserts, large cities and small towns. Which to prefer?

My preference didn't matter one bit, so I held on to the words of Ignatius: "I want and I choose what better leads to God's deepening life in me."

_____

Which of Ignatius's pairs of opposites do you find most challenging? Spend some time in prayer considering how you've experienced the spectrum between the extremes. In your own words, express your trust in God and your desire to be less attached to particular outcomes.

WEEK TWO:

VINEYARDS

LAGUARDIA ~ FUENMAYOR ~ NAVARRETE ~
LOGROÑO ~ ALFARO ~ TUDELA ~ ZARAGOZA

Tactics of the Enemy

Perhaps Ignatius's greatest contribution to our understanding of the spiritual life is his concept of the "discernment of spirits." He wants us to learn to listen for the voice of God—hearing that loving murmur through the din of all the other voices around us. The most pernicious of those voices Ignatius calls the "evil spirit" or the "enemy of our nature." Although not everyone is comfortable with the language of embodied evil—Satan conspiring against us—we've all experienced that disheartening pull away from being our best selves. Ignatius's clever analogies here help us notice how we get tripped up, and how we might resist.

IN HIS OWN WORDS:

Through three images we can understand better the way in which the evil spirit works.

The evil spirit often behaves like a spoiled child. If a person is firm with such a child, the child gives up his petulant ways. But if a person shows indulgence or weakness in any way, the child is merciless in getting his own way by stomping his feet or by false displays of affection. So our tactics must include firmness in dealing with the evil spirit in our lives.

The evil spirit's behavior can also be compared to a false lover. The false lover uses other people for his own selfish ends, and so he uses people like objects at his disposal or as his playthings for entertainment and good times. He usually suggests that the so-called intimacy of the relationship be kept secret because he is afraid that his duplicity will become known. So the evil spirit often acts in order to keep his own suggestions and temptations secret, and our tactics must be to bring out into the light of day such suggestions to our confessor or director or superior.

The evil spirit can also work like a shrewd army commander, who carefully maps out the tactics of attack at weak points of the defense. He knows that weakness is found in two ways: (a) the weakness of fragility or unpreparedness, and (b) the weakness of complacent strength, which is pride. The evil spirit's attacks come against us at both of these points of weakness. The first kind of weakness is less serious in that we more readily acknowledge our need and cry out for help to the Lord. The second kind is far more serious and more devastating in its effect upon us, so that it is a more favored tactic of the evil spirit.

—Spiritual Exercises of Saint Ignatius Loyola #325–327

CHAPTER EIGHTEEN
Be the Sweetness

How sweet are your words to my taste,
sweeter than honey to my mouth!

—Psalm 119:103 (NRSVCE)

The transition from Santa Cruz to Laguardia was so dramatic, it was hard to believe the two were within walking distance. We shifted from mountains into vineyards, and from the Basque region (with its strange, guttural tongue) into La Rioja (where we were more likely to hear Spanish). Since leaving Loyola, we had stayed in a series of villages; now we were in a bona fide town. Having awakened in a pilgrims' shelter, we'd be turning in for the night in a lovely hotel.

Like so many places we visited, Laguardia is rich with history. It once was a military fort defending the Kingdom of Navarre, but its medieval walls now provide a scenic overlook for the vineyards, while tunnels that sheltered women and children during battle have been transformed into wine cellars. We checked into the Hotel Marixa and relaxed over dinner in a private dining room with a spectacular sunset view. Before checkout the next morning, we enjoyed a walking tour that included a visit to a winery called *El Fabulista* (The Fabulist). Nothing prepares you for a ten-mile hike like starting the day with a wine-tasting!

In Laguardia, we bid farewell to Fr. Nilson, who would be quickening his steps for the rest of the journey. I was grateful for the slip-and-fall that had led to our spending part of the previous day's hike in conversation. Though Nilson assured us we'd meet again in Manresa, it was a sad parting; everyone would miss his youthful energy and steady good cheer. He left us with an encouraging word, observing that, when he looked at our little pilgrim band, he could see behind us the great many people who would be blessed by our pilgrimage.

Eyeing the vineyards from above, I gave thanks for the easier terrain: no more clambering over rocks. Our winding path sloped away from the walled city, descending gradually for a few miles before crossing the Ebro River and ascending a bit to Fuenmayor, our destination for the day. That looked great on paper, but I hadn't anticipated a new companion: shin splints.

I was downright hobbled. Every step was painful, and I watched in dismay as the group accelerated away from me. Days earlier, someone had quoted the motto, "If you want to go fast, go alone; if you want to go far, go together." I recalled that saying as I caught occasional glimpses of my fellow pilgrims around distant bends. Here I was, neither speedy nor accompanied, but decidedly slow and alone. Mentally, I began putting out drinks and snacks for my pity party.

Unexpected footsteps sounded behind me; perhaps my angst had been premature? This had happened once in the mountains, when I'd become convinced that I had fallen far behind the pack. *I really need to re-tie my boots,* I'd fumed, *but heaven forbid I pause the extra forty seconds to do that; I might lose the trail and never find it again. I wonder how far the group will get before anyone notices I'm gone. Maybe I should sit here on the side of this path and see how long it takes them to come looking for me.* Oh, the drama! A few minutes later, I'd rounded a bend and stumbled upon half the pilgrims, resting. Where were the other half? Behind me.

I shook my head, recalling a passage in the *Spiritual Exercises* about how we get tripped up by the evil spirit. "Like a shrewd army commander," Ignatius wrote, the enemy of our nature "carefully maps out the tactic of attack at weak points in the defense." Not being able to keep up with the others, I realized, had revealed a gap in my spiritual defenses through which great bouts of self-pity had come rushing.

Buck up, honey, I told myself. *Let's see who's coming.*

Oh, rats; it was Fr. José. He must have been hanging back to brighten up the Camino arrows with his handy can of orange spray paint, but now he was gaining on me fast. I braced myself for his familiar "Come on, pilgrim," knowing that I was incapable of any additional speed. *What if there were a bear behind you?* I challenged myself. Answer? *Then I'd be eaten—and could stop walking!* (It was a rough day.)

Coming alongside me, Fr. José did not criticize my pace. Instead, he simply said, "Would you like some grapes?" and extended one of the two dark, tiny bunches he had gleaned from the edge of a post-harvest vineyard. (In the weeks to come, the priest would glean figs, apples, pears, and even persimmons for our benefit.) I accepted the fruit gratefully and he lengthened his stride, quickly disappearing from view.

After a brief hesitation—*Wait, we're not washing these?* —I chewed the grapes slowly, savoring one miniature wonder at a time. As I trudged the last mile, I realized that every grape I enjoyed took my mind off my gripes. For whole moments, I was not thinking about my shins, and the walking grew easier.

As sweet as the fruit was, I mused, Fr. José's gesture had been even sweeter. (It was not the last time I'd be the beneficiary of his spontaneous kindness.) My mind began to rummage back over the week, remembering other sweet moments in our group. I thought about the morning when Tony had taken it upon himself to keep an eye on me on a challenging hill. Tony is a soft-spoken, intellectually curious actuary who is passionate about the connections among theology, economics, law, and business ethics; already, we'd had some fascinating conversations. At the moment, though, we were still in silence, so he quietly paced his steps to mine, pausing whenever I halted to gasp for breath. (Later, I told him, "In a movie, footsteps in the woods that stop when you stop are horrifying, but on the Camino, they're holy!")

Everywhere we went, I realized, sweetness had abounded. Pilgrims shared painkillers, cough drops, hats, nuts, chocolate, and advice. Pairing off as we walked, we shared the hard stories of our lives: stories of bereavement, of illness and diminishment, of drug-addicted loved ones, and of the search for meaningful direction after setbacks. (I was moved to learn that three of the ten women had been widowed.) Each tender encounter took our minds off our own pain.

Reflecting on this abundance of spontaneous kindness, I recalled a favorite quote from Catherine McAuley, the founder of the Sisters of Mercy. "There are three things which the poor prize more highly than gold," she wrote, "though they cost the donor nothing. Among these are the kind word, the gentle, compassionate look, and the faithful hearing of their sorrows." Catherine was speaking of the materially poor of her day (nineteenth-century Dublin), but the same wisdom applies to those who are experiencing any kind of physical, emotional, or spiritual lack today—and it still costs the donor nothing.

Beginning with the grapes and inspired by my fellow pilgrims, I began clinging to a simple motto: *Be the Sweetness.* People are laboring under so many burdens—only some of which we can see. Why not look for opportunities to be a simple touch of sweetness for someone else?

When we reached Fuenmayor, Beth-Anne loaned me a muscle roller stick to massage my aching legs. (I'm glad I wasn't the only pilgrim to make room in her luggage for comfort items!) It was as close to a magic wand as I was likely to get. Though the shin splints didn't vanish completely, they never incapacitated me again.

Sweetness had sent self-pity packing . . . for now.

When have you experienced a touch of sweetness in your life? For whom can you Be the Sweetness today?

CHAPTER NINETEEN
The Distress of the Vulnerable

I am the true vine, and my Father is the vine grower.

—John 15:1 (NABRE)

Do you know why those roses are there?"

I wouldn't have noticed the roses at all, if Fr. José hadn't stopped to point out one cheerful, unseasonable yellow blossom. But sure enough, each row of the reddening autumn vineyard was capped by a rose bush. He explained that roses are particularly sensitive to disease and pests, so they serve as canaries-in-a-coal-mine for the grape vines. If something is distressing the roses, that means it's coming for the grapes, and the vine grower knows to take protective measures.

After a week of meditating on the beauty of creation and God's tender love for us, we were turning our minds to the *Exercises'* exploration of sin—in ourselves and in our world. I found myself thinking about those roses, pondering the fact that their vulnerability is what makes them valuable. Just imagine if we could regard vulnerable *people* that way!

"Are there ways in which I have habitually not listened to those in need who have crossed my path?" Inspired by this question in my pilgrim's book, I tried examining my conscience through the lens of the roses: When had I failed to be attentive to the vulnerability of others? When had I lacked compassion for people who couldn't learn as quickly or work as efficiently as I could? Literally or metaphorically, how often had I sped past someone in need, aggravated rather than moved?

Taking the analogy a step farther, it occurred to me that many kinds of sin—from personal to global—can be described as a choice to ignore the distress of the vulnerable. Climate change comes first for people in poor nations, and toxic pollution for people in poor neighborhoods, allowing those of us who live elsewhere to remain blithely attached to our comforts. CEOs can safely ignore the distress of their stakeholders as long as their shareholders stay happy. Countless political and financial policies make things harder and more expensive for those who are poor, yet easier and cheaper for those who have more. Over and over, the distress of the vulnerable is at best ignored, at worst derided. (After all, isn't it their fault they're not strong like us?) I asked God to let the roses become my teachers.

As we continued our daily hikes through the vineyards, the yellow rose lingered in my imagination, helping me notice how attentive and compassionate the members of our group were to whatever weaknesses arose from day to day. Everyone remained exceptionally kind and patient, no matter which of us was "Paddy Last" arriving at a rendezvous point, or who merited the Bad Pilgrim of the Day award (usually given for a violation of some unwritten protocol, like deciding to go hunting in one's backpack *after* everyone else was strapped up and ready to move again.) Seeing my companions cheer when I topped a hill, rather than sigh and check their watches, made me grateful for their generous response to my vulnerability. If all the members of the body of pilgrims had been equally matched—all fit, strong, and independent—would we have had such a powerful experience of community?

In an email exchange after we returned home, Dave shared a humorous anecdote about vulnerability. Doing his morning stretches one day on the Camino, he noticed that three of his toes were badly blistered. Addressing the other seven, he joked, "You guys are going to have to do the work today"—as though the afflicted ones could just go along for the ride. Funny as this was, it reminded me of the serious advice Dave had given me when I had shin splints in Laguardia: *Let the big muscles in your legs and butt do the work on steep grades.* The stronger parts could compensate for the weaker ones, but if I failed to respond to the distress of those vulnerable little muscles, no part of my body was going anywhere (except for a ride in the luggage van). The truth of that simple observation radiated out: individually, communally, globally. We are profoundly interconnected.

"I am the true vine, and my Father is the vine grower," Jesus said. Now that I have gotten my sneakers dusty among the vineyards of La Rioja, I can more easily imagine God the Vine Grower, deliberately planting the vulnerable among the strong, so that all may thrive.

Who are the vulnerable people in your life, or in your circle of concern? How do you recognize and respond to their distress? How might you be more tender toward your own vulnerability?

CHAPTER TWENTY

Now, Where Did I Leave That Comfort Zone?

*"Therefore I tell you, do not worry about your life, what you will eat
or what you will drink, or about your body, what you will wear.
Is not life more than food and the body more than clothing?"*

—Matthew 6:25 (NRSVCE)

A lot of times we stop to rest in places with bathrooms, but other
times we don't. In those cases, normally we go in the bushes . . .
men in one direction, women in the other." That detail hit my inbox
in February of 2020 in response to a question I'd asked a woman who
had made the Camino before. *(What exactly is the bathroom situation—
especially for the ladies?)* Like so many realities of the pilgrimage, that
information lingered in my possession for two years without sinking in.
I simply could not picture myself plunging into bushes with a bunch of
women for a collective urination. I couldn't even get my head around
the mechanics. (Did I mention my knees don't bend like they used to?)

Although the veteran pilgrim had given us much helpful advice, her
recollection that "a lot of times" we would stop in places with bathrooms
is a testament to the unreliability of memory. Though we did occasionally
get to take a break in a roadside café or a park with public restrooms, those
delightful oases were the exception, not the rule. The rule, according to
Fr. José, was this: *If you see a town coming, find a bush before we get there.*
As the days wore on, he got to know us well enough to stop in strategic
locations, point dramatically, and announce "Ladies, that way!"

I waited my turn to slip behind whatever protective covering
presented itself until a day in our second week when Fr. José directed
the women up a wooded path and I *really* had to go. Flinging modesty
aside, I joined them and discovered it was more private than I'd feared,
as everyone maintained "custody of the eyes." From that day on, I was
a convert, gladly joining the other women as we found creative places

to relieve ourselves. On our final hike, we headed into the trees and prepared to get busy, only to hear Fr. José sing out, "I can still see you!" I sang back, "Then turn around!" What a difference a few weeks had made.

I was shoved out of my comfort zone for good when we arrived in Fuenmayor and Fr. José ushered us into an unoccupied day care center. "Find your suitcase," he ordered, indicating the heap of transported luggage, "get what you need to shower, and follow me." A strange parade ensued, as we made our way through town carrying towels, toiletries, and changes of clothes. When we reached the recreation center, the women queued up outside the ladies' shower room, then in we all went together: one big room, many shower nozzles.

I had never showered in a group. Ever. My high school didn't have a serious gym requirement; I hadn't played sports or even gone to summer camp. My family had been so modest that I was almost entirely unfamiliar with other women's bodies. *What was I going to do?*

Get in the shower, that's what. After a stunned moment in which we all considered just how much closer we were about to get, the women burst out laughing and shrugged out of our dusty hiking clothes. There weren't enough nozzles for everyone to shower at once, so half of us huddled in skimpy towels waiting our turn. (Someone who shall remain nameless had forgotten hers; another woman kindly pumped long sheets of paper towel from the dispenser for her to cover and later dry herself with—yet another sweet moment between pilgrims.) The whole escapade was so ridiculous and unexpected; we shrieked with helpless laughter for the duration. After we dressed and rejoined the men in the lobby, they pointed out that we sounded like we'd had much more fun than they did. (Later, I learned that the men's shower room had private stalls. I might have been envious at the time, but in retrospect I wouldn't trade the women's definitive bonding experience.)

Back at the day care center, we explored our lodging for the night. There were two connected rooms with air mattresses on the floor, so the men took the first, smaller one, while the women moved into the larger room beyond. This meant that the women would need to pick our way back through the men's dormitory in the dark—guided only by the cacophony of their snoring—if we wanted to use the bathroom overnight. And I do mean *the* bathroom; there was only one for our whole group, plus a room of tiny training potties. Neither door had a lock, so we set toy bowling pins in front of each to signal "occupied." Fortunately, we made it to the next morning's departure without anyone barging in on anyone else.

I look back on our stay in Fuenmayor with great fondness. While my recollection may be tinged with the rosy glow of memory, one of the things that really surprised me about myself on the Camino was how easily I rolled with the more "edgy" lodging (which grew even edgier two nights later in Logroño, where we shared one big bunk room with strangers). The farther from my comfort zone I was dragged, it seemed, the more accepting I became. Though I wasn't consciously praying "God, grant me the serenity to accept the things I cannot change," serenity is the best word for what washed over me in both Fuenmayor and Logroño. Instead of being tempted to fuss about what our lodging lacked, I found myself grateful for what I had—like the warm sleeping bag ordinarily over-stuffing my suitcase.

Though I was familiar with Victor Frankl's words about the last freedom being "the ability to choose one's attitude in any given set of circumstances," the Camino made me realize that my own rigidity was *creating* the hard edges of my comfort zone. This attitude is such a sharp contrast to what Fr. José often reminded us: "We have God; there's nothing else we need."

Now, when life stretches me uncomfortably, I try to practice the spirit of serenity that sustained me along the Way. I don't always succeed, but if I can pee in the woods with a light heart, anything is possible!

How capacious is your comfort zone? When have you stepped—or been nudged or shoved—out of it? What did you learn about yourself there?

CHAPTER TWENTY-ONE

Caring Less

Whatever town you enter and they welcome you,
eat what is set before you.

—Luke 10:8 (NABRE)

We bid farewell to Fuenmayor and walked less than four miles to the fortified city of Navarrete. There, we intersected with the French route of the *Camino de Santiago*; we began seeing its scallop shell markers as well as many more pilgrims (who often inquired worriedly if we were lost, as we were headed the "wrong" way—east rather than west). In the parish hall of Our Lady of the Assumption, we settled in for our first group meeting since Loyola. "Talk about how it's been going," Fr. José invited.

It was gratifying to hear what had been unfolding for people in the silence. We started by naming the stressors of the journey—from the comforts we missed to the quirks of our aging bodies—but quickly pivoted to the graces we were experiencing. At the top of the list was the grace of simplification: with so few decisions to make or external distractions (especially of the electronic variety), life had narrowed down to what was right in front of us—and what was going on inside us. This focus was enriched by our two hours of silence each day, a universal source of delight. When someone described it as "emptying the mind rather than filling it," Fr. José concurred. He encouraged us to maintain what he called the pilgrim's "wandering mind," accepting whatever bubbled to the surface as material for prayer. We mused that every moment of each day could provide matter for reflection—which, of course, was true in "ordinary" life as well. Perhaps that's what Mama Jane meant when she said the pilgrimage experience was like having "a jolly good personal trainer!"

As I thought about my own progress over the last several days, one of the things I noticed was that—as hoped—I'd managed to relinquish my leadership to Fr. José without continuing to feel responsible for everyone's pilgrimage. Though I still fielded the occasional question, or summarized Fr. José's logistical instructions on our WhatsApp thread, I didn't let those tasks preoccupy me. From the moment we stepped onto that bus in Barcelona, I was content to be one pilgrim among many, offering my gifts while relying on those of others. What a relief.

The sharing could have continued for hours if it hadn't been time for Mass and our midday meal, after which—miracle of miracles—we were *on our own* until breakfast the next morning. It was the most liberty we'd had in over a week.

Beyond the physical rigors, the most challenging aspect of the Camino was having so little *choice* for such a long time. Not since childhood had I less control over what I ate or wore, how I spent my days, where I lay my head at night, or when I needed to be up and out the next morning. Fortunately, that also meant I didn't have to waste time thinking about those superficial things; this constraint freed my attention for deeper realities. Though unnerving at the outset, simplicity of choice proved to be a hidden luxury of the Camino, liberating me from the tyranny of my own picky preferences. But I noticed that my attachment to my own desires resurfaced, disappointingly, whenever I regained even a bit of control. This would be one of those days.

We were staying in *La Posada Ignatius*, a hotel that had once been the palace of the Duke of Nájera, where Ignatius had spent three years in service before the Battle of Pamplona diverted him from swashbuckling to sainthood. I could imagine a youthful Iñigo taking the wide stone steps two at a time, dagger flashing below his flamboyant attire. A sign in the foyer advertised "pilgrims' massages" (an unexpected benefit of the better-traveled route), but Porter and I chose a nap followed by a trip to the pharmacy to stock up on blister supplies. I looked forward to a rare early night.

Or not. Jim was a veteran of several pilgrimages with his wife, Evelyn, along the *Camino de Santiago*. For days, he had been reminiscing about a tapas joint in Navarrete that he was excited to share with us, so at eight o'clock (early by Spanish dinner standards) we made our way to *Bar Deportivo*, a few blocks from the hotel. In my imagination, we were going to pop in for a glass of Tempranillo and a couple small bites. In reality, owner Antonio was so delighted to be remembered that he set up a special table for us in the courtyard, where he brought out waves of delicious food: appetizers, a mozzarella salad, roasted vegetables, coffee, dessert. As my desired bedtime came and went, I grew restless. This was not what I expected!

No, it was *better*, silly—an opportunity to enjoy something deservedly special to one of our new friends. We lingered, and chatted, and lingered some more. My attachment to what I thought I wanted yielded to the joy of the moment.

A few years ago, I read a novel in which a wealthy woman always ordered a replacement entree if she didn't love her first selection, because "life is too short to be disappointed by things you can control." This strikes me as the antithesis of Camino wisdom. I'm not Goldilocks; not everything needs to be "just right." It doesn't matter whether my eggs are scrambled or fried, or which movie we stream on a Saturday night. I don't need to figure out exactly what I want at every single turn.

Wanting tethers our brains to the future. *How much longer will we be walking uphill? When do we stop for lunch? Is there a washing machine at the next hostel?* On the Camino, these and countless other questions (stemming from obvious wants) popped into our heads and flew out of our mouths all day long, but Fr. José kept encouraging us to stay focused on the *now*. This path. These companions. This moment. This prayer. These smells and sounds and sights and feelings. He was teaching us to unhook our minds from a preoccupation with what *might be*, to be fully present to what was right in front of us, and to welcome with open hearts whatever came our way.

Now that I am home and get to (have to) decide every blessed thing for myself, it is easy for those superficial wants to clamor for attention again. The internet estimates that we make up to thirty-five thousand decisions a day. What would it look like to approach those choices with the heart of a pilgrim? (And if more of us did, how might that change the world?)

Although my greatest pet peeve is people saying "I could care less" when they mean the opposite, *caring less* is now my aspiration. I'm talking about nonessentials here—matters of simple preference. Regarding important choices, Ignatian spirituality calls us to careful discernment and the cultivation of fruitful habits. But when it comes to the little stuff, I hope that *caring less* will create the mental space I need to care more about the big stuff—and free the energy I need to put that care into practice.

That night in Navarrete, I thought I wanted a solid eight hours' sleep. I got a treasured memory instead. Morning found me on the Way again, striving to be present to my fellow pilgrims, to the unfolding landscape, to the movements of my own heart and, through it all, to God.

What choices have you made today? In the last hour? What guided those choices? Going forward, try to notice what attachments motivate your wants. Could you care less?

CHAPTER TWENTY-TWO

God Is Bigger Than Our Worst Mistakes

But where sin abounded, grace did much more abound.

—Romans 5:20 (KJV)

The next two days held unexpected graces—starting with my ability to walk more energetically on the new, flatter terrain. My body was changing, getting used to the distances; I even showed up near the front of the pack from time to time. As our meditation on sin continued, I was glad for the head space to think of something other than my feet.

Outside of Navarrete, when we circled up to pray before our two hours of silence, I found myself looking at the scar on Porter's neck where an enlarged lymph node had been removed five years earlier. That scar became my entry point for the morning's prayerful rumination.

Following a biopsy, our local hospital had diagnosed Porter with Hodgkin's lymphoma. In the course of staging the lymphoma, they discovered his bladder cancer, which demanded a more urgent course of treatment. Having two apparently unrelated malignancies made us flee to the well-regarded Fox Chase Cancer Center, who ran their own pathology tests and discovered that Porter did *not,* in fact, have lymphoma. They called the lump on his neck a "proliferative adenopathy" (which I believe is Latin for "we don't know, but we're not worried").

Ordinarily, a misdiagnosis could be grounds for a medical malpractice suit. And yet, if not for the full-body scans needed to stage the pseudo-lymphoma, Porter's real cancer would not have been detected until it became symptomatic—far more advanced, and difficult to treat. That medical error may have saved his life (or at least his quality of life). I cherish the mark on Porter's neck because it reminds me of how close we came to a darker path.

Some mistakes leave permanent scars, I reflected, *but that's not necessarily a bad thing.* Ignatius's limp, for example, must have been a constant reminder of his terrible decision at the Battle of Pamplona. "My sin is always before me," King David sang in his beautiful, penitential Psalm 51. Did those words resonate for Ignatius as well? If so, I hope he kept praying the psalm all the way to the end, for it continues, "You will let me hear gladness and joy; the bones you have crushed will rejoice" (NABRE). Though David was speaking metaphorically, Ignatius's actual bones had been crushed by the French cannonball. That injury—a downfall brought about by his own grandiosity—opened the door to unfathomable goodness, for himself and for the world. Such is the mystery of God, who is bigger than our worst mistakes.

Keeping our sin before us was the order of the day, but not to wallow in remorse. Rather, like Ignatius, we were invited to let the awareness of our sin lead to an even greater awareness of God's mercy.

As if on cue, a chain link fence appeared, into which people had woven hundreds of crosses made of twigs and bits of bark. For several minutes, we walked in silence along this spontaneous shrine. I tried to imagine the pilgrims on the Way of St. James who had placed them there. Each person must have paused, searching the ground for appropriate materials before pressing them carefully through the fence. What sins had brought them to their knees? What knowledge of forgiveness had raised them up again? Despite the rumble of highway traffic, that fence was a profoundly holy place.

After Navarrete came Logroño and the pilgrims' shelter *Albas,* where we'd be sharing a bunk room with strangers—another departure from the comfort zone. It had been a short walk from Logroño—only ten miles—so we were the first to arrive. Ezekiel, the upbeat innkeeper, greeted us warmly, then doubled as waiter for both dinner and breakfast at his brother's restaurant next door.

Fr. José instructed us to fill in from the back to leave bunks near the door for late arrivals and warned us about the strict quiet/lights-out policy from ten p.m. to eight a.m. (points of pilgrims' shelter etiquette we hadn't needed to know when it was just us). For the first time, our men and women did not bunk separately; Porter and I found ourselves opposite Beth-Anne and Canada Jane. Everyone gave each other the privacy they needed, though, and afterwards we agreed we'd all been very good neighbors.

I wasn't sure what to expect from the strangers, but they were young and mostly kept to themselves. Nevertheless, I passed on navigating the showers, deciding for the only time on the Camino that bathing was overrated. Instead, before dinner I sat at the kitchen table next to Fr. José, each of us seizing the opportunity to get some writing done. Looking up from his laptop, he peered over at the journal entry appearing on my iPhone screen. "Too tiny!" he exclaimed. "I could never write on that." Screen size was a trade-off he was not willing to make, even in the service of traveling lightly.

But speaking of trade-offs: glancing up, I spotted an electric kettle and a jar of instant coffee on a shelf. Aha! I might not smell great in the morning, but at least I could omit the daily wrangle with my immersion heater in the dark.

The following night's lodging was at a hotel in Alfaro; it was too far to walk, so we got to experience our first train ride. Fr. José pushed us at a good clip that day, since missing the train would have been disastrous (or at least unfortunate, as another was not due for hours).

We needn't have worried—or rushed quite so much. We reached the train station at Alcandre with ninety minutes to spare. It was just an overhang with a few benches, so people began settling themselves as best they could for the long wait—except for Tony, who approached Fr. José with a gleam in his eye. "There's a church up that hill; mind if I pop over and see if it's open?" Porter and I laughed; was that dear man never tired? Incapable of popping anywhere, we stretched out on the concrete platform in the sun. Hats over our faces, we fell sound asleep.

When we reached the hotel, we spent almost an hour tending to one another's feet. Dual blisters now bracketed each of my heels, and the ball of Porter's right foot was one big hot spot; I had trouble finding a bandage wide enough to cover it. Presently, the group headed back out for Mass and a visit to the nearby church of Our Lady of Burgo, which has the routes of the intersecting Caminos etched in glass on the doors.

It was all beautiful, but a lot of walking, and we didn't reach the hotel for dinner until after what I would have considered bedtime.

As happy as I'd been to have my mind off my feet earlier, they were pretty much all I could think about that night. Recriminations started slipping in through the cracks of exhaustion. Why was I not better prepared for this? I had all the information . . . the distances, the altitudes. I had three *years* to find good shoes, yet here I was, trapped in Spain with two disappointing pairs. I knew hills were hard for me, but I never once took myself to the gym—a thing I pay for every month—to do the elliptical or stair climber or leg machine. I kept saying I wanted to do training walks, yet in the end the most I'd pulled off was a few jaunts of eight flat miles apiece. I could have wept with frustration—if I weren't so tired!

Although I wouldn't go so far as to call my lack of preparation *sinful,* rarely have I been so profoundly disappointed in myself. I knew I needed to pray with these emotions but didn't want to go there while I was feeling so flayed.

God is bigger than our worst mistakes, I reminded myself. Perhaps things would look brighter in the morning.

―――――――――――――

What scars (literal or figurative) have the mistakes of your past left on you? Can you behold any beauty in them because of something that has come about as a result? Ponder the astounding goodness of God, who is so much bigger than our worst mistakes.

CHAPTER TWENTY-THREE
Failure Is Not an Option

Come to me, all you who labor and are burdened,
and I will give you rest.

—Matthew 11:28 (NABRE)

I awakened in Alfaro conscious only of weariness and discouragement. I wanted to be present to the whole Camino experience, but physical afflictions were narrowing my field of vision. From bed, I flipped through the notes on my phone to words I had written in my application almost three years earlier. There, I shared my fear that uncertainty and discomfort would "preoccupy me beyond their ability to teach me."

Well, at least I'd brought self-knowledge.

From the beginning, I had understood that challenges were an integral part of the pilgrimage—the very things through which I would stretch, grow, and above all, learn. But I sensed there was a tipping point beyond which misery would no longer be instructive, and wondered anxiously on which side of the balance I would land.

The answer seemed clear later that afternoon as I hobbled into Tudela, completely undone by our sixteen-mile hike. The walk had started out so well—we'd even paused for a coffee break at a square in Castejón after only an hour. I should have known we were in trouble when Fr. José pointed to the public fountain and instructed us to fill up, as this would be our last water source. What sort of terrain has no water for thirteen miles?

We spent the rest of the day hiking under a sun as unforgiving as the stony landscape, pausing only to sit on the ground and eat our lunch in the gravelly shadow of an abandoned building. Civilization was nowhere to be found. At one point, Fr. José dragged us across a crunchy field so we could catch a glimpse of the Ebro River, but none of us could spare the extra steps to get any closer.

As the afternoon wore on, we looked for ways to raise one another's flagging spirits. I found myself in a conversation about the Bible with

Dave's wife, Karen, which inspired me to narrate the plots of two of my dramatic interpretations of women in Scripture. That bought us a couple of miles. Then the conversation took an uncharacteristically silly turn, as some of the women began inventing Camino-themed lyrics to the tune of a military cadence. I resurrected "The Other Day I Met a Bear," a childhood call-and-response song, but couldn't remember how it ended. Eventually, we ran out of diversions, trudging along in a grim silence that was nothing like the morning's prayerful solitude until we reached the outskirts of Tudela.

Ana had intended to ride with the luggage van that day; like Veronica, she had developed painful sciatica. But a sudden change of heart had propelled her out the door on foot instead, giving her ample time to regret her decision. When we emerged at last onto an actual road, the poor woman was bent double, half-carried by Fr. José and Charlie on either side, while other pilgrims toted her pack and walking sticks. A quick phone call revealed that the closest cab was twenty minutes away, so the priest flagged down a passing motorist to take Ana to our destination. (I'll admit I was a bit envious of her ride!)

As was his custom, Fr. José took us on a brief tour through town en route to our hotel. I was desperate to be off my feet, but someday I hope to revisit the cathedral in Tudela. Its highlight is a thirteenth-century "judgment gate" with an enormous, intricately carved stone arch. The right side includes fifty images—simultaneously gruesome and comical—depicting the torments of hell in punishment for particular sins. (There are images of heaven on the left side, but they're not nearly as interesting.) Gazing up, I felt something pop on the underside of my left foot. I gasped in pain; it was like one of those little demons had come down off the archway to torment me—but for what offense?

Reaching our hotel room at last, I removed my boots and discovered that I now had *seven* blisters—including one that had rendered a baby toe unrecognizable—so I decided to name them. The four nipping at my heels became Fido, Rex, Max, and Fifi; the ones under the ball of each foot Doom and Gloom, and the baby toe Napoleon, as befitted a little tyrant. Meanwhile, Porter's hot spot had morphed into one giant bloody blister. We asked Karen, a physician's assistant, to give us a hand; she was rewarded for her kindness by being squirted in the face by Napoleon!

(A few hours earlier, she had been exploring an unusual plant when it fired a liquid that aggravated her skin; this was not Karen's day for fluids.)

After dinner, Porter and I told Fr. José we didn't think we could handle the next walk, and he ordered us to take off our shoes, examining our feet right there in the dining room. (Fortunately, we pilgrims were the only patrons.) After much headshaking, he brought us up to his room and did extensive blister repair with his own first-aid kit—while concurring that the following day's hike was probably not a good idea. We could take the train to Zaragoza instead, where a rare free day awaited the group.

From bed the next morning, I realized that uncertainty and discomfort had, in fact, preoccupied me beyond their ability to teach me. Our pilgrim's book said we should be meditating on Jesus's invitation to walk beside him in his work; how was I supposed to do that if I couldn't walk at all? Even though I knew Ignatius said we should not fix our desires on success or failure, this experience of defeat was overwhelming—especially since much of it could have been avoided if I'd secured proper footwear and hiked more hills. I sent an anguished email to my spiritual director, lamenting, "I failed to prepare well, and now I'm at risk of 'failing' the Camino."

Susan's response was swift and firm. "You cannot fail the Camino if you truly see it as a spiritual quest," she insisted. "Let go of all the hopes and musings and imaginings that preceded the reality of what is happening and open yourself to what is being offered through the reality of what is happening." With that, she swept the categories of "success" and "failure" off the table.

I realized that the despair I was feeling probably signaled some shenanigans on the part of the evil spirit. This sent me back to a sermon of Pope Francis from the day we gathered in Loyola, which I'd bookmarked on my phone. Speaking of how we "password protect" sensitive information in our financial lives, the Pope suggested that the spiritual life also has passwords, ones that lead straight to our hearts. "The tempter, that is, the devil, knows these passwords well," he said, "and it's important that we know them too, so as not to find ourselves where we do not want to be." Pope Francis wasn't only speaking of winding up on the wrong side of the Judgment Gate. Anything that distracts us from God's desire for us can be considered a temptation.

I realized I'd been tempted to grade myself as if I were still in school—Pass/Fail, A through F—with mastery defined by miles walked and lessons learned. Ironically, this shortsightedness put me in good company with the man whose footsteps we were following. In *Ignatius of Loyola: the Pilgrim Saint*, biographer José Ignacio Tellechea Idígoras describes the future saint's early faith as being marked by "imitating the external idiosyncrasies" of the saints who inspired him, "obsessed with notions of *doing* great things rather than enduring or experiencing them." But there was no such thing as getting a 4.0 in pilgrimage—not for the saint, and certainly not for me. There was only, as Susan said and as Ignatius learned, the reality of what was happening, day by day, hour by hour.

Only by opening myself to that experience could I discover what was being offered me there. The temptation to measure myself harshly was exactly that—a temptation, luring me away from a true encounter with God in the present moment.

If the "what-ifs" are a leading temptation, the "might-have-beens" are a close runner-up. Can you remember a time when your mental image of what something would be like blocked you from appreciating the real thing? If you are wrestling with a disappointment, prayerfully try to open yourself to the grace of what is being offered—right there in the reality of what is happening.

CHAPTER TWENTY-FOUR

Letting the Mule Decide

*The donkey saw the angel of the LORD standing in the road,
with a drawn sword in his hand; so the donkey turned off the road.*

—Numbers 22:23 (NRSVCE)

The only thing I regretted about having to skip the walk to Zaragoza was that I wouldn't get to visit the statue depicting my favorite Ignatius story.

Here's how it goes: Somewhere along his pilgrimage (in Luceni, if the statue is to be believed), the newly converted Iñigo struck up a conversation with a man he refers to in his *Autobiography* simply as "a Moor." Along the way, they had an animated conversation about things of faith, which turned, eventually, to the question of the Blessed Mother's perpetual virginity. The Muslim gentleman professed his belief in Mary's virginal *conception* of Jesus—the real miracle, however you look at it—but could not accept that she'd remained a virgin after Jesus's birth. Nothing Iñigo said could persuade him, so they parted ways. The Moor spurred his horse, leaving our poor hero to rehash the argument as he plodded along on his mule.

Try to set aside any eye-rolling about the topic of their debate. For Iñigo, it was a point of honor—*his Lady's* honor, which, he feared, he had failed to defend adequately. Awash in the default emotions of his early conversion—shame and anger—he debated catching up with the Moor to "give him a taste of his dagger." Unable to figure out whether God preferred that he *kill or not kill* the stranger, Iñigo resolved to let his mule decide. As he approached the fork in the road where their paths should have diverged, he dropped the reins. Would the mule follow the broad path the Moor had taken, to the man's peril, or would it stick to the less traveled route Iñigo had intended?

Like the donkey commonly referred to as "Balaam's ass" in the Book of Numbers, the beast of burden resisted the path of folly—a path that might have turned Iñigo into a murderer instead of a saint. Did God intervene, as in the Scripture, sending a sword-wielding angel visible only to four-footed eyes? We'll never know.

What we do know is that Iñigo was possessed of a conscience so inadequately formed that only the wisdom of a mule saved him from making a terrible (and, to us, obviously sinful) choice. That his conscience continued to mature is a testament to the slow and steady work of God, inspiring patience with ourselves and with one another. The man who entrusted a critical life decision to a dumb animal is now known for his wise teaching on the practice of discernment. Perhaps that experience convinced him that there had to be a better way to search for God's will.

Throughout the month, as we walked the route that Iñigo's mule had trod, we modern-day pilgrims shared the stories of our lives, often discussing the discernment that had preceded key turning points. Some of my longest conversations happened with Dave, the Director of IVC New England. At seventy-nine, he was (by almost a decade) the oldest member of the group that started in Loyola. Frequently, he kept me company at the back of the pack—though, unlike me, Dave and his blistered toes walked every step of the Way. Calling ourselves The Turtles, we frequently sustained each other with wide-ranging "turtle talks."

One of the discernment stories Dave shared sounded ridiculous at first blush. When he was faced with one of the most important vocational decisions of his life, he recounted, a good friend had advised him to flip a coin. *Seriously? Was there not a mule handy?* The friend's seemingly bizarre advice had a (mature) Ignatian spin, however. Don't just flip the coin. Flip it—then notice how you feel when it lands. You may think you're completely torn, but if you find yourself either relieved or disappointed, you've gained valuable insight.

Dave's friend's idea is actually an abbreviated version of a process Ignatius himself recommended in the *Exercises*. Given a choice between two good options, he suggested, bring your imagination to bear on first one possibility, then the other, noticing whether you feel consolation or desolation in the wake of your imagining. The deepest desires of our hearts are one with God's desires for us, Ignatius believed. Anything that helps bring those desires to the surface can be a useful exercise.

Sorry as I was to miss the statue of Ignatius and the Moor parting ways, it was clear that I would not be walking to Zaragoza. Fortunately, I knew that my deep desire for the Camino was not about walking all the miles, but about growing closer to God. Before falling asleep, in my journal I wrote, *Since my stupid left foot seems to be the deciding mule right now, I guess my* attitude *is the only thing I can control.*

Even when circumstances dictate our decisions, there is always room for discernment.

It's easy to rib Ignatius over the mule incident, but I suspect we often toss the metaphorical reins to someone or something else, fearing to choose poorly. When have you outsourced responsibility for a decision instead of using your own discernment? On the other hand, when has yielding to circumstances beyond your control drawn you closer to God? What does this tell you?

CHAPTER TWENTY-FIVE

Pausing

*In vain do you get up early
and put off going to bed,
working hard to earn a living;
for he provides for his beloved,
even when they sleep.*

—Psalm 127:2 (CJB)

There's an old tale in which Himalayan sherpas (or, in another version, African tribesmen) are hired by a group of American trekkers to transport their supplies. After a few days of walking fast and far, the locals sit down and refuse to move for several hours—waiting, it's explained, for their souls to catch up with their bodies. Although I didn't have the liberty of such on-the-spot refusal along the Camino, I did come to appreciate the power of the pause.

My longest was the three days I spent in the city of Zaragoza. On a Monday morning, Porter and I caught the train from Tudela, ensconced ourselves in a café so I could write for a while, then walked slowly to the Hotel Sauce. Doing our best to approach this wide-open day with wide-open spirits, we lingered wherever we saw something interesting. We stopped in a hardware store for a carabiner to secure the straps of Porter's old suitcase and visited a department store—*El Corte Inglés*—to invest in new hiking socks. That brief stroll recalled us to ourselves, reminding us how much we enjoy exploring a new city. It also helped us see beyond our transitory struggles, anchoring us in the surpassing goodness of our life together.

Despite our having a free day on Tuesday, by Wednesday morning my feet were still awful, and Porter was feverish—felled by the slow-moving stomach virus that had been making its way through the group. We would have to linger in Zaragoza for one more day. Our hotel room had a bathtub with a broad ledge at one end, allowing me to indulge in two refreshing pastimes while Porter slept: soaking my feet and perusing the *New Yorker* magazine I'd optimistically chucked in my suitcase.

There, I became absorbed in an article about adventure travel that shot me back to my questions about what constitutes a "real" Camino. In "Only Disconnect," Ed Caesar narrates having been dropped solo in the remote mountains of Morocco, challenged to use his wits (and GPS) to reach a set destination. The experience—for which he'd paid good money—had been alternately strenuous, frightening, and exhilarating. Only when it was over did he discover that the "Get Lost" support team had been tracking him from five hundred yards back the whole time. Caesar's departure from his comfort zone had been more extreme than ours, but it, too, had balanced uncertainty with security. Though admitting the artifice of what he calls the "luxury of living for a short while under the illusion that I was [disconnected]," he nevertheless found his hike deeply gratifying. As with our pilgrimage, Caesar's external journey had been meaningful only as a catalyst for his internal one. Like us, he did not want the experience to end.

Late that afternoon, I made a long, solo visit to the Basilica of *Nuestra Señora del Pilar*—Our Lady of the Pillar. This Basilica was even grander than the stone fortress of Arantzazu, and its origins even more the stuff of legend. When St. James began evangelizing the Iberian peninsula in the first century, the story goes (preaching the Gospel "to the ends of the earth"), he almost despaired of bringing the Christian faith to that pagan land. One day, while he was deep in prayer along the banks of the Ebro River, the Blessed Mother appeared to him atop a rosy pillar, encouraging him not to forsake his mission.

The cavernous interior of the Basilica houses an intimate chapel where a tiny Mary statue sits atop a pillar of pink jasper. Even though the Basilica felt cold and empty, the chapel was warm with the devotion of many visitors; I was lucky to witness a weekly ceremony where children receive a special blessing and get their picture taken with the statue. Pausing in prayer, I felt something shift in me; heading back to the hotel, I realized that I was walking much more easily. Like the apostle James in that same place almost two millennia ago, I felt a renewed hopefulness and a readiness to rejoin my friends on the road the next morning.

Though the three-day break in Zaragoza was a great blessing, pauses did not need to be long to be restorative. On our steepest climbs, when the grade was fierce, I allowed myself to stop for a few deep breaths every ten steps. Count to ten; stop and breathe. Count to ten; stop and breathe. In addition to getting much-needed oxygen to my lungs and leg muscles, this strategy kept hope in view. I knew that in seven . . . five . . . three more steps, I could take a brief, blissful pause, until the terrain grew merciful, and I could press on without stopping.

The most delightful pauses arrived unexpectedly. Occasionally, as we walked through the woods, a clearing would open and—voilà—a café where we could grab a quick *cortado* and use real restrooms. Fr. José never told us they were coming. This was consistent with his desire to keep us in the present moment, though I suspect he also relished being able to offer us a pleasant surprise. Those periodic oases of rest lasted just long enough to refill my well of gratitude before starting out again.

Perhaps my insight here seems obvious. *Take a break;* do you really need me to tell you this? But maybe you do; maybe, like me, you tend to soldier on. Maybe you never take a sick day (or didn't, until COVID made bringing your germs to work seem less heroic). Maybe you wouldn't dream of closing your eyes for five minutes after lunch. Maybe you stare at the Sunday crossword puzzle long after your brain has stopped generating solutions, or routinely accept diminishing returns for your labor in exchange for the ego boost you get from thinking of yourself as a person who "never quits."

So, in case you do need to hear it, I'll say it again: *There is power in the pause.* Whether for a moment or an hour, a day or a week, a well-timed pause can reconnect us to ourselves, giving us fresh energy and perspective. More importantly, the pause can reconnect us to God—inventor of the Sabbath, after all—for whom accomplishment is never everything.

You know who knew this? Jesus. He routinely slipped away from a life of preaching and miracle-working to pause, pray, and recharge. "Come to me, all who labor and find life burdensome, and I will give you *rest,*" he said—not "and I'll give you more to do!" Holy pausing is not about taking the easy way out or shirking our share of life's burdens. It's about acknowledging our utter dependence on God, who alone provides strength for the journey.

In what circumstances do you tend to soldier on? What's that about, do you think? How might you carve a restorative pause into your next busy day, week, or season?

CHAPTER TWENTY-SIX

Stopping

Though my flesh and my heart fail,
God is the rock of my heart, my portion forever.

—Psalm 73:26 (NABRE)

My spiritual director says you can't fail the Camino as long as you're seeing it as a spiritual quest." I'd been hanging onto this advice like a life preserver, and now I tossed it to Ana, who had pulled me aside after dinner in Zaragoza. Struggling even before her crippling sciatica outside Tudela, Ana was trying to decide whether to call it quits. I thought she might cling to Susan's words for a few days as she discerned her next steps, but in the morning, Ana was gone. She caught a train to Barcelona, rescheduled her flight, and headed home.

It's not that Ana wasn't finding goodness on the Camino. She had made it to Day Fourteen—the midpoint of our pilgrimage. During group reflections, she shared how much she'd enjoyed getting to know the other pilgrims, and how moved and humbled she'd been by the judgement-free help we'd extended. But it was clear that she was not experiencing our adventure as any kind of "spiritual quest," just an excruciating and potentially dangerous endurance test. Mindful of her full life back in the States—meaningful volunteer work to pursue, delightful grandchildren to mind—she decided to leave early. Completing the Camino was not as important as her physical and emotional well-being.

.There is an image in the *Spiritual Exercises* that I've always loved: a balance at equilibrium. This is how Ignatius says we should be before making a decision about something significant. "I find myself like a balance at equilibrium," he wrote, "ready to follow whatever I perceive to be more for the glory and praise of God our Lord and the salvation of my soul." Note that he didn't say "ready to stick with whatever I already decided" or "ready to follow whatever makes me look best in the eyes of others." Such attachments often skew our decision-making.

In my thirties, for example, I spent several semesters working on a post-master's certificate in spiritual direction, taking one evening a week away from my campus ministry job to attend classes. Plate too full, I found myself skimming the assigned reading, conscious that my just-get-through-it attitude wouldn't fly once the practicum part of the program began. It hadn't crossed my mind to do anything but persevere, until I participated in a prayer exercise planned by a fellow student. Suddenly, a liberating certainty washed over me: *I didn't have to do this anymore.* I left the program at the end of the semester, grateful for the wisdom and friends I'd gained through the experience.

Ignatius was clear that the occasion for decision-making is "insofar as we have a choice and are not bound by some obligation." And yet, even in the face of obligation, there is room—indeed, necessity—to listen for the voice of God.

I'm reminded of an evening of reflection when I performed my dramatic interpretation of the Woman at the Well from John's Gospel. A line that has always intrigued me in that story is when the Samaritan woman runs to tell her neighbors, "Come and see a man who told me *everything I have ever done*" (John 4:29, NRSVCE, emphasis mine). Although Jesus had revealed that he knew about her five marriages and irregular living arrangement, that hardly seems like "everything" she'd ever done. What else did Jesus say? In my imaginative rendition—which assumes that a woman of her day would not have been discarding husbands like yet-to-be-invented Kleenex—Jesus provides a compassionate backstory. Of husband number four, he says, *I know that he made your life a living hell, and the bravest thing you ever did was run away.* After the program, a woman approached me with tears in her eyes. "I did run away," she said. "And it took so much bravery."

We do not always recognize the outer limits of our own struggles—and we can be obstinately blind about the limits of others. By leaving early, did Ana "fail" the Camino? I don't think so. I think she walked with us for as long as she could, then made a life-affirming decision to change course.

Her choice reminded me of something I too often forget: sometimes, it's okay to stop.

———————

Have you ever reached the decision to end a commitment? (Notice I didn't say "quit," which connotes a hasty, unthinking departure.) Whether you left a position, team, relationship, organization, church, etc., I suspect the decision was not made lightly. When you sit with it in prayer, what feelings linger? Can you be at peace with what was and what is?

WEEK THREE:

DESERTS

BUJARALOZ ~ ALCARRÁS ~ LLEIDA
~ PALAU D'ANGLESOLA ~ VERDÚ
~ CERVERA ~ JORBA

Christ the King
and His Call

Ignatius frequently encourages us to use our imagination in prayer. In this meditation, he invites us to imagine the rousing rhetoric of an ideal earthly leader, followed by the even more compelling invitation of Christ. Although he begins by calling this exercise "the stuff of which fairy tales are made," Ignatius always sees imagination in the service of reality, bringing us into the intimate knowledge of Jesus that leads to a wholehearted commitment to his mission.

IN HIS OWN WORDS:

There are two unequal parts in this consideration, the first one naturally leading to the more important second part.

In the first part, let me put myself into a mythical situation—the kind of story-truth of which fairy tales are made. I imagine a human leader, selected and raised up by God our Lord himself; every man, woman, and child of good will is drawn to listen to such a leader and is inspired to follow his call.

His address to all men rings out in words like these: "I want to overcome all diseases, all poverty, all ignorance, all oppression and slavery—in short, all the enemies of mankind. Whoever wishes to join me in this undertaking must be content with the same food, drink, clothing, and so on, as mine. So, too, he must work with me by day, and watch with me by night, that as he has had a share in the toil with me, afterward he may share in the victory with me." If a leader so attractive and inspiring and so much a man of God makes such a call, what kind of person could refuse such an invitation? How could anyone not want to be part of so challenging and noble an adventure?

In the second part, I consider Jesus Christ our Lord and his call. If a human leader can have such an appeal to us, how much greater is the attraction of the God-Man, Jesus Christ, our Leader and King! His call goes out to the whole of mankind, yet he specially calls each person in a particular way. He makes the appeal: "It is my will to win over the whole world, to conquer sin, hatred, and death—all the enemies between mankind and God. Whoever wishes to join me in this mission must be willing to labor with me, so that by following me in suffering, he may follow me in glory."

With God inviting and with victory assured, how can anyone of right mind not give himself over to Jesus and his work?

Persons who are of great heart and are set on fire with zeal to follow Jesus Christ, eternal King and Lord of all, will not only offer themselves entirely for such a mission, but will act against anything that would make their response less total. They would want to express themselves in some such words as these:

"Eternal Lord and King of all creation, humbly I come before you. Knowing the support of Mary, your mother, and all your saints, I am moved by your grace to offer myself to you and to your work. I deeply desire to be with you in accepting all wrongs and all abuse and all poverty, both actual and spiritual—and I deliberately choose this, if it is for your greater service and praise. If you, my Lord and King, would so call and choose me, then take and receive me into such a way of life."

—*Spiritual Exercises of Saint Ignatius Loyola #92–98*

CHAPTER TWENTY-SEVEN

On the Road Again

At once the Spirit drove him out into the desert,
and he remained in the desert for forty days, tempted by Satan.

—Mark 1:12–13 (NABRE)

One of the items occupying precious real estate in my suitcase was a headlamp. I was beginning to think I'd packed it in vain—until we decided to leave Zaragoza three hours before sunrise.

Uncharacteristically, Fr. José had surprised us with a choice. We were going to be hiking across the plateau of the Monegros desert: would we like to begin under a starry sky and watch the sun come up as we walked, or start later? Even though it meant having breakfast at five o'clock, the pilgrims were excited to experience something so beautiful.

Unfortunately, thick cloud cover hid both stars and sunrise the next day. Nevertheless, the terrain was striking—nothing like my mental image of a desert (mostly derived from Bugs Bunny cartoons). The severe landscape stretched for miles, offering no protection from the elements. It had rained overnight, so the ground was more like sticky clay than sand, clinging to our boots at each step.

Just as it was time to break silence, Fr. José surprised us again by inviting us each to go find a place to pray in solitude for twenty minutes. I picked across the scrubby terrain until I found an open patch, then awkwardly maneuvered to the ground and set my phone timer. A piney fragrance caught my attention, and I realized I was surrounded by wild rosemary plants. (Also rabbit droppings.) Feeling a sharp wind slice across the plateau, I pulled my neck gaiter up like a bandana for warmth. Once I was as comfortable as I was likely to get, I began to pray.

We were moving into the Second Week of the *Exercises,* in which we contemplate Jesus's life and public ministry through a series of Gospel passages. The Monegros provided a perfect setting to pray with the story of Jesus's own desert experience. I imagined him heading into the desert after his baptism, driven by the Spirit to fast for forty days. There, he had wrestled with demons and pondered his mission. So many possibilities lay before him at the outset. *How many approaches to his ministry had Jesus considered and rejected?* I wondered. *Did the temptations he endured in the desert clarify his thinking?*

Like Jesus, I realized, I was going to be walking out of this desert—this pilgrimage—with decisions to make. My ministry is multifaceted: I write books, lead retreats, help with IVC programming, and volunteer in my parish. Any one of those commitments could consume my time, but I had left campus ministry so my time would no longer be consumed. *In this uncharted territory,* I mused, *how is God calling me to proceed?* The answer to that question would unfold gradually, I knew. I had to trust that the Spirit who had driven me into the desert would show me the way forward as well.

A rustle of chimes from my phone summoned me, and I rose reluctantly. Although I had come to appreciate walking prayer, I missed the stillness of extended contemplation. I felt a pang of longing for the Jesuit Center for Spiritual Growth in Wernersville PA, my spiritual home for over three decades, which had closed a year earlier. *Mental note,* I thought, as I shouldered my backpack: *Don't sacrifice your favorite prayer just because you can't return to your favorite place.*

When we emerged from the desert, the bar/restaurant *Venta de Santa Lucía* stood like a sentinel on the empty highway. Having set out early, we arrived before it opened, so we passed the time cleaning the mud off our boots by splashing about in puddles and finding sticks to pry the larger chunks out of our treads. People began sharing snacks. Having been on the receiving end of much sweetness, I was glad to be able to offer a paper bag full of candied pear I'd bought during my rest day in Zaragoza.

The bus that would take us on the last leg of our journey was still five hours away, so, after the traditional midday feast, we ensconced ourselves at tables in the bar. Karen took off her boots and doctored her blisters discreetly. Some people caught up on reading their pilgrim's book or writing in their journal, but many seized the opportunity to rest.

There's a funny picture of us looking like obedient schoolchildren with our heads down on our desks, sound asleep.

At the appointed hour, we went outside to meet the bus. Two of our companions, still weakened by the stomach bug, were riding it all the way from Zaragoza, but didn't realize we'd be joining them for the tail end. When the driver pulled off the road to pick up our raggedy crew, they leaped out to greet us as we stowed our backpacks in the external luggage compartment.

In Bujaraloz, the *Hostel El Español* was like nothing I'd experienced: our rooms occupied the second floor of a truck stop with a 24-hour buffet! Fr. José handed out keys and told us when to meet in the lobby for dinner. As we climbed the stairs, I joked that I hoped he wouldn't mind if I came down in my socks, as the firm backs of my ordinarily comfortable orthotic sandals just tortured my blisters. Canada Jane whirled around, asking, "What size are your feet?" I gratefully accepted the hot pink flip-flops she'd picked up in Barcelona "just in case," which I sported every evening for the rest of the trip. Once again, the Camino had provided—through the generosity of another pilgrim.

When we regathered in the lobby, a few of our number were missing, as they'd gone into the buffet already. Fr. José had a rare comic meltdown. "Pilgrims!" he pleaded. "When I say meet me *here,* do I mean *over there?* I do not! There are about to be ten more of you; you must be the *very best pilgrims!*" He was right: when we reached Lleida, this poor priest would have two dozen of us cats to herd. We seasoned pilgrims had to get our act together!

Lying in my twin bed that night, hearing faint music from the still-hopping buffet downstairs, I gave thanks for a truly memorable day. The pain in my feet had been far outmatched by fellowship and prayer.

It was good to be on the road again.

As a metaphor, the desert is a place of solitude and searching, testing and trial, where the absence of comfort creates a space for the presence of what really matters. Ideally, the desert is a place we choose to go, but often, life thrusts us there. Have you ever had a desert experience? What did you learn?

CHAPTER TWENTY-EIGHT

Examen

You sift through my travels and my rest;
with all my ways you are familiar.

—Psalm 139:3 (NABRE)

Although Fr. José gave us points for reflection each morning—condensing the buffet of readings in our pilgrim's books to a nourishing morsel—somewhere along the way I took to beginning each walk by recalling the previous day, using a form of Ignatian prayer called the Examen. This is short for "examination of consciousness," a simple five-step prayer that Ignatius considered an essential component of the spiritual life. I'd learned about the Examen in college, and tried sporadically to practice it over the decades, but only in recent years have I come to love it. The reason it took so long is embarrassing: I was in my fifties before I realized I didn't have to pray it at *night*. Some people follow the saint's timetable literally, pausing at midday and again in the evening, but for me, embracing the Examen happened when I realized I could pray it first thing in the morning. That's my time of day—and anything I can't recall about yesterday probably isn't worth remembering anyway.

At home, my best chance of praying the Examen well is if I can do it upon arising, sitting in my rocking chair with a cup of strong coffee, gazing at the still-dark sky. Shortly before the Camino, I discovered another way. Minding a dog for a few days, I found that the time it takes to give a furry friend a little morning walk was just right for the classic Examen. I also realized that walking—as opposed to sitting—was a good way to savor the prayer without fighting the urge to hop up and do something "productive."

The pilgrimage took my walking Examen to a whole new level, however. Even though Ignatius said the prayer should take no longer than fifteen minutes, on the Camino I sometimes devoted up to an hour, wringing every drop of grace from the previous day. Though I tried to record careful notes each evening, often I was too tired to capture any more than bullet points on my phone. Literally walking through the

Examen's steps of gratitude, light, rumination, contrition, and hope each morning helped me view the last day through a spiritual lens instead of getting stuck on the physical level.

Another reason it took me decades to embrace the Examen is that, as a younger person, I kept reducing the Consciousness Examen to an *examination of conscience*, falling into bed at night and thinking, "Okay, what did I do wrong today?" No wonder it held little appeal! Even though a good Examen includes contrition and sorrow, that's not the goal. The purpose of the Examen is to help us wake up—to be attentive to the reality of God's invitations through the minutiae of our days. If I can be still—or walk quietly—long enough to notice where God was yesterday, I'm more likely to notice where God is today, and respond accordingly.

If you want to try this prayer, here's how I approach it:

Step One: Gratitude. I give thanks to God for whatever occurs to me: big things like health, faith, and love; small things like the fresh morning air or a chorus of birdsong in the trees.

Step Two: Light. I ask the Holy Spirit to enlighten my memories, showing me what I most need to see about the period under consideration.

Step Three: Rumination. I play back the previous day in my mind like a movie, pressing PAUSE on whatever moments feel significant. Intensity of emotion is a clue, but sometimes a seemingly insignificant detail will resurface, inviting me to go deeper. *Where was God in all this?*

Step Four: Contrition. I notice where I have missed the mark. Expressing my sorrow to God, I consider whether I also owe an apology to someone else and think about how I can do better.

Step Five: Hope. I look to the day ahead. What will it hold (to the best of my knowledge)? What challenges do I anticipate? I set an intention to be more responsive to God through the particulars of the coming day.

If you are new at this, try not to be put off by struggling to learn the "rules." (What were those five steps again?) There are many helpful resources out there. But to be clear: there's no need to make five perfectly executed steps. The Examen is simply about recollecting ourselves, trusting that we can find God in the midst of an ordinary day—or an extraordinary one.

———————————————

Whether or not you are already a friend of the Examen, consider taking a few minutes—or a short walk—to practice the steps, and notice what surfaces.

CHAPTER TWENTY-NINE

Standards

No one can serve two masters.
He will either hate one and love the other,
or be devoted to one and despise the other.
You cannot serve God and mammon.

—Matthew 6:24 (NABRE)

The nicest thing about sleeping above a 24-hour buffet is that you don't have to make your own coffee in the morning. When my alarm buzzed in Bujaraloz, I slid a few coins into the pocket of my sweatpants and slipped downstairs, treating myself to a morning *cortado*. Gathered around the breakfast counter were men in some kind of public works uniform, supplementing their coffee with shots of liquor. Whether they were coming off a night shift or fortifying themselves for the day ahead, I do not know. Add that to the enduring mysteries of the Camino!

As we began our thirteen-mile walk, I felt like I was into the swing of it at last. My feet hurt, but not tragically, and the rest of my body was cooperating. Though repacking my suitcase and hurling myself out the door each day would remain a challenge to the end, getting on the road and entering the silence had begun to feel like coming home.

Fr. José usually waited until we reached the outskirts of town before pausing to lay out the reflection points for the day ahead, concluding with a spontaneous prayer. I came to love the sound of his gently accented voice entrusting our day to God. After we sang our verse of "The Servant Song," silence would settle around us as we began to walk. He encouraged us to begin with *Good morning, God!*—a practice that I and many of my fellow pilgrims have continued with delight back at home. Setting out, I felt a wave of joy wash over me. *Well, good morning,* I prayed. *Here we are again!*

The suggested text that day was "Two Standards," a key meditation from the *Spiritual Exercises*. Two meanings are at play. Today, we think of "standards" as criteria of excellence, but the Spanish word is *banderas*: banners carried into battle (as in "standard-bearer"). Ignatius the courtier-turned-military-man used this imagery—familiar to his century, if less so to ours—to capture the essence of his conversion. Previously, he had marched under the standard of an earthly king; he knew the surge of self-obliterating loyalty that led men to follow such a ruler into the fray. But now he took his marching orders from Christ the King—a far more worthy leader who inspired a different kind of sacrifice.

In "Two Standards," Ignatius presents the banner of Christ as set against that of Satan—the enemy of our human nature—and invites us to consider the stakes. The evil spirit, he proposes, leads us to covet worldly riches and gain public honor, which leads to the vice of pride. By contrast, the way of Jesus leads us to desire spiritual poverty (a humble awareness that every breath is a gift from God) and accept material poverty. This opens us to the contempt of others, which leads to the virtue of humility. From riches and honor to pride, or from poverty and contempt to humility: these are the paths Ignatius foresees, depending upon whose banner one chooses to march under. For readers unmoved by military imagery, the other sense of the English word "standards" also applies: do we measure ourselves by worldly or godly ones?

I decided to explore the trajectory of my own life. As I walked, I asked myself: *do I covet earthly riches?* I want to be a person who embraces simple living, yet I can't deny that I own a lot of stuff. The word "covet" is a clue. What is my attitude toward my possessions? Do I use them to help others? Could I let go of them if that's where God's Spirit were leading me? I decided to figure out how much I donated to charity each month versus what I spent on fitness; doing the mental math, I was relieved to discover that my recurring charitable donations edged out the cost of my gym membership and Pilates lessons—though barely. I made a note to reevaluate my spending when I got home, both to eliminate frivolities and to be attentive to where God might be calling me to generosity.

Following the downward path, I next considered "honors" and "pride." It is the nature of my work to be in the spotlight. I'm often the one in the front of the room, speaking on retreats or cantoring in church—heck, you're reading my book right now! So, the question, again, is about motivation. Ignatius said we should do all things *ad majorem Dei gloriam* (for the greater glory of God)—a motto so compelling that "AMDG" is still common parlance in Jesuit circles. Am I putting myself out there to garner accolades, or am I allowing myself to be, in St. Teresa of Calcutta's words, a simple "pencil in God's hand"? (Not even a pen!) *Be faithful to your call,* I encouraged myself, *but be sure to polish other people's gifts, so they too can shine.*

My several miles of mulling over the Standards did not yield any dramatic revelations. I simply prayed for three things: the ability to notice the motivations of my heart; freedom from "inordinate attachments" to riches, honors, and pride; and the grace to orient my actions AMDG—for the greater glory of God.

At a hostel in Alcarrás that evening, the fifteen of us gathered around a long table. The next day, we would reach Lleida and expand our number, so Fr. José invited us to reflect on the coming transition.

It was bittersweet. There were about to be joyful reunions, as many of us had friends in the incoming crowd. But widening our circle would mean losing the smaller group's established intimacy. Although most of us hadn't met until that dinner at *Ocho Patas,* our shared experience over mountains, vineyards, and deserts had drawn us close. How would the dynamic change? Would our tender, budding friendships be neglected in favor of old, established ones? This was particularly poignant for those who didn't know any of the new people.

For seventeen days, our pilgrim band had been striving to walk more faithfully under the standard of Jesus—the one who said, "I was a stranger, and you welcomed me." The spiritual task now at hand was clear: to welcome the arriving pilgrims, while doing our best to ensure that *no one* felt like a stranger.

*Riches . . . Honor . . . Pride . . . Poverty . . . Contempt . . . Humility
. . . As you ponder those words, what feelings arise? Talk with God about
which you desire. Or perhaps you could try an artistic prayer exercise:
literally drawing the two "standards" in competition for your loyalty.
What symbols would you put on each?*

CHAPTER THIRTY
Just One Thing

There is need of only one thing.
—Luke 10:42 (NRSVCE)

The skies were threatening as we left Alcarràs, so we donned our rain gear before heading out the door. A little wet weather couldn't dampen my spirits, though—Rose and Carmen were already checked into the Hotel Real in Lleida. We'd be together by lunchtime, as the city was only nine miles away! I chuckled, remembering when that would have felt like a long walk. By the time I'd worked up a sweat under my plastic poncho, the clouds had scattered.

Prayer that morning took me to two of my favorite Gospel passages: "Martha and Mary" in Luke and "The Rich Man" in Mark. Each involves an invitation to discipleship beyond the comfort zone. In the first, Jesus invites a harried hostess to abandon her anxious worry and focus on the *one thing needed*. In the second, he invites an earnest seeker to move beyond the security of "commandments kept" and embrace the *one thing lacking*—selling what he has, giving to the poor, and following.

Each story ends on a moment of suspense. *What happened next?* Did Martha sit with her sister and listen to Jesus while dinner grew cold in the kitchen, or did she storm off in a huff at his reprimand? When the rich man "went away sad, for he had many possessions," was he distraught about not being able to follow Jesus, or about having to get rid of all that stuff? Each story captures a moment in time but—like us—the real human beings had the rest of their lives to figure out their one thing: how to respond more faithfully to Jesus's calling.

As I prayed with these characters, I discovered a connection among us. Jesus called each of them into freedom—Martha to be less bound by her busyness, the rich man to be less fettered to his possessions. I, too, have experienced that call. My freelance work has been a liberating invitation to use my best gifts in the service of God's people—to focus on my own *one thing*, yet I'd begun worrying that the transformation wrought by the Camino might send me in a new, more difficult direction. But then I realized that, whatever came next for Martha or the rich man, following Jesus would have been a joy, not a burden. I had to trust that this would be true for me as well, no matter what the future held.

As our prayer ended, the pilgrims gathered briefly in the courtyard of a small church, then followed the Segre River toward Lleida. A distinctive cathedral tower marks the skyline, so we'd been able to see the city for an hour already when we crossed the bridge. For the first time since Zaragoza, we were walking along busy streets: dodging pedestrians and ogling store windows. We entered the walled "old town" and checked into our hotel, glad to have a few free hours before the all-pilgrims rendezvous. Using WhatsApp, I connected with Rose and Carmen, who agreed to find us a lunch spot. After a quick round of foot care and sink laundry, Porter and I headed out to find them.

What a delight! A few blocks from the hotel, there was Carmen, keeping watch for us, while Rose held a table inside. They had already ordered tapas, so we had no decisions to make. We yelped with joy and clung to each other. After years of planning and weeks of messages from the road, there we were, sitting in a restaurant with our dear friends.

At five o'clock that afternoon, the sidewalk outside the Hotel Real was abuzz with pilgrims greeting old friends and introducing new ones. Our most delighted arrival was Mary McGinnity, IVC's President and CEO, whose dream of an IVC-sponsored pilgrimage finally had come to fruition. Fr. José led us to the parish of St. Ignatius, where we gathered in a big circle for introductions, then celebrated Mass before heading back to the hotel for dinner. Our already-long table had grown much longer!

Go to bed, Fr. José urged us after dinner. The new pilgrims would not be easing in, as a hot fifteen-mile walk awaited us. For the moment, the one thing necessary was a good night's sleep.

What's your "one thing"? How is God calling you to use your best gifts in service of others?

CHAPTER THIRTY-ONE

Crucible

Out of the depths I cry to you, O LORD.

—Psalm 130:1 (NRSVCE)

To say that the arriving pilgrims would not be *easing in* was the mother of all understatements. Perhaps it was unwise to begin during the Third Week of the *Exercises,* when we reflect on Jesus's passion and death? Our pilgrim's books encouraged us to "pray for the grace of experiencing Christ's own anguish as our own." Watch what you wish for!

The newcomers included two people in their seventies and two in their eighties. Like the rest of us, the group varied in both fitness and preparedness, and the pace caught many of them by surprise. Spain was having its worst October heat wave in more than a hundred years. Although the terrain was fairly flat, it offered little shade; for the first time, sunburn became a risk. One person suffered from digestive distress—everyone's worst-case scenario on the trail—and others had respiratory issues brought on by poor air quality. *Three times* that day, Fr. José had to call the emergency vehicle to pick up an ailing pilgrim where the dirt path crossed a paved road.

As awful as this was for them, there was an upside for me: I was no longer trailing the pack. Two and a half weeks of walking had strengthened my legs and my lungs. Though I still couldn't keep up with many of the pilgrims, now I didn't have to; I could hang back like Fr. Nilson to bolster the spirits of the stragglers.

Our lunch that day was at a restaurant unlike any I've experienced in the United States: a fancy establishment attached to a gas station. Two long, linen-covered tables awaited us, where we enjoyed several courses accompanied by the traditional midday bottles of red wine. I knew better than to indulge when we still had miles to walk, but I dug into the entree—pasta with shellfish and a delicious garlic aioli. Easing my boots off under the table, I pushed away thoughts of the remaining hike and simply appreciated the food and conversation.

By the time we reached Palau d'Anglesola, however, I understood why Fr. José wanted us to move at a decent clip: we'd been on the road for nine and a half hours. The "back of the Slinky" was moving much slower than it had during the previous two weeks. Each time the group had to stop and wait, the day lengthened.

We arrived at last at the *Pensión Sant Antoni,* a quirky old building with varied sleeping configurations. Porter and I lucked out, sharing a room with a twin bed and a cot, while many others were either solo or tripled. Showering would have to wait, though; we had to spin it around quickly, as we were on the verge of being late for a meeting with the mayor. He turned out to be a young guy in jeans and a tee shirt, looking more like a grad student in philosophy than a public official. He welcomed us warmly, then someone from the tourist office showed a video about how the residents of Palau d'Anglesola offer respite to those traveling both the *Camino de Santiago* and the Ignatian Way. Before we left, they gifted us a bottle of wine and a platter of regional sweets. As exhausted as we were, it was moving to see the pride these people took in the hospitality of their tiny town.

Across the narrow street from our *pensión* was a small restaurant where we gathered for dinner after the mayor's welcome. When the salad course arrived, I took only a few bites before needing to find a restroom. Returning to the table, I looked at the food and realized I couldn't stay. Excusing myself, I ducked back into the hotel and proceeded to be sick for the rest of the night. Had the roving virus caught up to me at last, or was it the rich lunch fare? I'll never know—but it will be a long time before I slather garlic aioli on my pasta again. (Later, I learned that the dinner entree had been whole fish; if I hadn't departed early, the sight of an eyeball staring up at me might have sent me over the edge anyway.)

Though I can remember nothing from that morning's prayer—having been too sick by nightfall to capture any notes—what I do know about that crucible of a day is that it bonded our enlarged group more quickly than any easier outing would have. For example, when we reached the lunch restaurant, several of our party were missing. Mama Jane asked me, "Do you have any idea where my husband is?" Looking around, I speculated. "Well, Fr. José hung back to wait for the transport vehicle. Rose is probably helping, because she's a nurse. Carmen always helps Rose, and Tony helps *everyone,* so that must be where he is." Sure enough, when the helpers reached the restaurant, we learned that Carmen and Tony had practically carried an ailing companion the last mile to the public road. (There's a great picture of Tony grinning in the entrance to his namesake *pensión,* the *Sant Antoni;* we joked that his saintly reputation had preceded him.) Even beyond these heroic efforts, everyone was unfailingly patient and caring throughout our very long day, rallying to provide support to those who needed it.

Once again, the distress of the vulnerable had brought out the best in the rest of us.

There's nothing like a hard time to pull people together. When have you experienced this? Were you the one helping, or the one being helped? Either way, can you savor the goodness—the God-ness—in the midst of the storm?

CHAPTER THIRTY-TWO

Rest

I think of you upon my bed,
I remember you through the watches of the night.
You indeed are my savior,
and in the shadow of your wings I shout for joy.

—Psalm 63:7–8 (NABRE)

In the morning, it was clear that I couldn't walk to Verdú—I had a fever, and was so washed out, I wasn't sure I could make it to the corner. I remembered how upset I had been when I was unable to walk to Zaragoza, and marveled at the level of peace I was feeling now. I had learned my lesson: *Do not ignore the distress of your own vulnerability!*

Three of us would be traveling with the luggage transport that day. We brought our suitcases to the lobby, bidding the group farewell as the drivers wedged all the bags into a trailer. The two men headed across the street to grab breakfast, so we settled down to wait. Unable to keep my eyes open, I curled up on one of the couches and pulled a blanket over me. Two and a half hours later, the men reappeared. Either it was the world's most leisurely breakfast or there had been some sort of Spanish-to-English communication breakdown. (My money's on "B.")

Half an hour later, we arrived in Verdú at a pilgrims' shelter called *Sant Pere Claver.* (We were in Catalunya now; *Sant Pere* is Catalan for the Spanish *San Pedro*—Saint Peter Claver in English.) Though most of the rooms were on the second and third floors, the entrance level included one room with three bunk beds. Declaring it "the infirmary," we each claimed a bottom bunk, and I fell sound asleep again. Later, knowing that we needed nourishment, we ventured out the door and discovered a little *tienda* halfway down the block, where I bought instant chicken soup and a Coke. In my luggage, I still had a clear plastic tub of Saltine-type crackers I'd purchased when Porter was sick. For the rest of the afternoon, I alternated between sipping soup or soda, nibbling on crackers, and sleeping. By the time our friends arrived, I felt a bit human again.

I'm so glad I didn't have to miss that evening's outing to Peter Claver's birthplace; we toured the home, watched a documentary about his life, and celebrated Mass in the chapel. I hadn't known much about this saint before the Camino, but his story is inspiring.

Born in 1580, he entered the Jesuits at the age of twenty-two and was assigned to a Jesuit college on the Spanish island of Mallorca. There he encountered a doorkeeper, Alfonso Rodriguez, SJ (also later canonized), who encouraged him to minister in the Americas. Claver arrived in what is now Colombia in 1610—a truly dreadful era in the slave trade. Declaring himself "slave of the black slaves forever," the saint dedicated himself to the physical and spiritual well-being of those arriving on galley ships. He did this work for forty-four years—often to the derision of local and even church authorities. Claver died at the age of seventy-four, weakened by an illness that was exacerbated by the neglect of the person assigned to care for him. He was canonized in 1888 by Pope Leo XIII, who said that since the life of Christ, no life had moved him as deeply.

After Mass, we walked from the saint's birthplace to his home parish, the Church of Santa Maria. Behind the altar, Fr. José pointed out a crucifix graphically depicting the agony of Christ, and explained that Claver's desire to ease the pain of enslaved people had had deep roots. Gazing at this crucifix throughout his early years, he said, Claver had felt the agony of Christ and longed to relieve it. After the suggestion of that humble doorkeeper, his desire found expression in a life of passionate self-sacrifice in Cartagena.

Fr. José contrasted this somber cross with a different image of Jesus that he'd shown us back at the Jesuit church in Zaragoza. The crucifix known as the "smiling Christ" originally hung in the castle of Javier, Spain—the childhood home of one of Ignatius's closest companions, Francisco de Javier (known to us as St. Francis Xavier). In this depiction, Jesus looks positively serene, even joyful. Fr. José speculated about how such an image might have imprinted itself on the young Francisco, who grew up to be the first Jesuit missionary, serving in India and Japan until his death at age forty-six. "This Jesus," Fr. José said, "is smiling because he is giving over his life—it is not being taken from him. Remembering that crucifix, Francisco Javier might have thought, 'If I am going to be like You, Jesus, then what is the problem? I give myself—whatever happens!'"

Sitting in the Church of Santa Maria, I thought about the power of religious imagery. I remembered the church in Legazpi, where a statue of Jesus laid in the tomb showed his knees split open right to the bone, as well as many crucifixes I'd seen in Mexico City graphically depicting the torture Jesus endured. Then I pictured the crucifixes at the front of so many American churches, where Jesus looks like he is resting comfortably or even resurrecting triumphantly. How does this form the spirituality of the Christians who gaze on those white-washed images?

We returned to the pilgrims' shelter, where the staff had provided sandwiches for our dinner. That was beyond my fragile stomach's capacity, so I decided to crawl back into bed. But I wound up chatting with one person, then another and another, wandering around with my little tub of crackers. Before I knew it, folks were pulling chairs into a circle; apparently, Fr. José had called a group meeting. Shoot! I'd missed the chance to sneak off to sleep.

There were twenty-five of us now. How long would this meeting last? If everyone spoke for five minutes, it would run over two hours. I needn't have worried, though; Fr. José is such a deft facilitator. He asked a simple question: *What one word would you use to describe how you are feeling right now?* When the first person answered, "Tired," Fr. José quickly modified his question: *What* other *word would you use?*

The meeting was short but touching. My own contribution is lost in the mist—and Porter had crashed early in the men's dormitory upstairs—but in my journal I noted that people said they felt graced, grateful, challenged, and all sorts of other good words. Once again, I was humbled to be in their company. Fr. José ended the meeting by describing the next day's eleven-mile walk, speaking of it so beautifully that I didn't want to be left behind. Though I was hard-pressed to imagine I'd be feeling well enough, suddenly I went from assuming I would ditch to hoping I could go.

Crawling back into my bunk, I prayed, *Whatever you want for me, Lord,* and drifted off in peace.

———————————

The spirituality of both Peter Claver and Francis Xavier was formed, in part, by the depiction of Christ in their home churches. Can you remember the religious imagery of your childhood? What effect did it have on you? Are there other images that speak to you more powerfully now? What do you think makes a religious image meaningful?

CHAPTER THIRTY-THREE

Resurrection

If the Spirit of the one who raised Jesus from the dead dwells in you, the one who raised Christ from the dead will give life to your mortal bodies also, through his Spirit that dwells in you.

—Romans 8:11 (NABRE)

I set out the next day with a low-grade fever, hoping I was not repeating Ana's mistake in Alfaro. Immediately, I began questioning the wisdom of my choice. My tummy was okay, but my feet were miserable.

We took advantage of public restrooms an hour later in a town called Tárrega. While I removed my boots to bandage my feet more effectively, Rose grilled me about pain management. I was embarrassed to admit that it hadn't occurred to me to take anything other than some Advil or Aleve at bedtime. Rose sighed, donned her invisible nurse's cap, and sternly advised a regimen of over-the-counter analgesics. The combination, dosage, and frequency were shocking—more than I'd ever taken at once. I'm not going to repeat her instructions here, lest anyone overdose themselves on my account. But Rose assured me that, while I should not attempt this at home, the most important thing at that moment was to get my pain under control.

What a game-changer! Within an hour of following her advice, my pain had subsided to a tolerable level, where it stayed for the rest of the hike—ten hot miles over gravelly roads. I was grateful for her advice but also for the hiking poles loaned to me by another new pilgrim, Ann. I'd broken one of mine and Porter had accidentally abandoned the other, but Ann had brought a borrowed pair that she was not finding helpful. Between the painkillers and the extra support, things were looking up.

Though we were still in the third week of our pilgrimage, our prayer had shifted to the Fourth Week of the *Spiritual Exercises,* in which we contemplate Jesus's resurrection and pray that we may enter fully into the joy of the risen Christ. As we began our period of silence, Fr. José urged us, "Let us feel in our senses that we are alive with Christ—alive with eternal life!"

I began by asking myself, *How have I experienced resurrection—life where life seemed impossible?* My mind raced to my improved feet, but quickly moved on to more profound resurrections. I gave thanks for the sobriety of someone dear to me, whose addictions had been life-threatening. Could I have dreamed, just a few years ago, that this person would be so well now? That's the "mystery" part of the paschal mystery—the suffering, death, and resurrection of Jesus that echoes in our own experience. To walk in the joy of the risen Christ, I reflected, is to walk with confidence in the unimaginable goodness God can bring forth in the most troubled life.

For several hours, we'd been able to see the walled town of Cervera on a distant hill. By the time we reached the outskirts, we were all pretty wrung out from the heat. There was a public water spigot, so I removed the purple bandanna adorning my backpack and drenched it, wiping my face and neck with the icy coolness. Those whose water bottles were empty filled up and drank thirstily. Fr. José spotted us and exclaimed, "What are you doing? That water's not potable!" Seeing the look on people's faces, he shrugged and said, "Well . . . everyone has to die from something." I have no idea if he was kidding—but am happy to report that no one died from Cervera water.

We climbed the steep, cobbled streets to our next pilgrims' shelter, a large former convent. After we dragged our suitcases up two flights of stairs—the elevator was out of order—we discovered yet another type of accommodation. The women's wing was a long corridor with tiny curtained-off cells whose partitioned walls did not reach the ceiling; our privacy would be visual, not auditory. Each room had its own sink, so I had the new experience of doing laundry while sitting on my bed!

That evening, we toured Our Lady of the *Sabinas* (Junipers). Elevated behind the altar was a solemn statue of the Blessed Mother sitting with the baby Jesus on her lap. Such prominent images of Mary had been a feature of many of the churches we'd visited (Our Lady of the Owls, of Arantzazu, etc.), but you rarely see such a central depiction of

Mary in the United States—even in churches bearing her name. Karen later wrote about how moving she found those images, which gave her a more immediate feeling of God's love radiating from mother to child. "I think it helped open my heart more," she said.

Another thing Our Lady of the Junipers had in common with many churches on our itinerary was the extensive damage the building had suffered in the 1930s during the Spanish Civil War. (The closer we got to Barcelona, the more often Fr. José started sentences with "Before the Spanish Civil War . . ." and went on to describe yet another treasure destroyed by left-wing forces.) One side altar stood out from the rest. Ornate and colorful, the altar of St. Andrew appeared to be several centuries older than all the others. Fr. José explained that a group of parishioners, getting wind of approaching vandals, had protected their favorite altar by walling it up with stone. This wasn't the first story we'd heard about heroic efforts to protect religious artifacts; apparently, the crucifix in St. Peter Claver's home church had been saved by parishioners who buried it in a wagon full of manure until the danger passed! It occurred to me that resurrecting these holy objects at the end of a devastating war must have felt like sharing the joy of the risen Christ.

We walked back to the pilgrims' shelter for dinner, pausing to peer down from the high walls of Cervera across the dark landscape. When Fr. José took the next day's lunch orders, the veterans seized the opportunity to extol the virtues of a tuna omelet sandwich. A twenty-mile hike awaited us, so we did not linger at table that night.

The distance between the men's and women's wings presented a challenge, again, for couples sharing supplies. In the cell next to me, Rose got a text from Carmen asking for something buried in her big suitcase. Not wanting to disturb her neighbors by rummaging, Rose brought the whole thing to the lounge between wings. She opened it and began searching, but stopped, perplexed by the alarmed expression on her husband's face. In the shadows, Fr. José was standing like a chaperone at a co-ed slumber party. "Rosemary." He sighed. "Go. To. *Bed.*"

Whatever Carmen needed out of that bag, Rose would have to resurrect it in the morning.

When have you experienced the "mystery" part of the Paschal Mystery—the confounding goodness that God can draw forth where there appeared to be nothing but ruin?

CHAPTER THIRTY-FOUR

Shortcut

On the day I called, you answered me;
you increased my strength of soul.

—Psalm 138:3 (NRSVCE)

When we left Cervera the next morning, I was still hobbling badly. Fearing to take that hefty dose of painkillers on an empty stomach, I'd waited too long. To make matters worse, I'd accidentally packed my headlamp, and it was still pitch dark. (Three weeks at this latitude, and I still couldn't get used to an 8:20 sunrise.) With only my iPhone flashlight for assistance, I picked my way down the steep, uneven cobblestones. The group accelerated past me, as usual. When they disappeared around a corner, I started to cry.

Months later, I read the following passage in Tellechea Idígoras's biography of Ignatius; it's from the saint's early days in Italy. *"Some of [Iñigo's] traveling companions went off to get a health certificate at Padua. He could not keep up with them because they walked too fast, and so they left him behind 'at nightfall in a vast field.' It was one of his worst experiences of total abandonment, and he tells us that here 'Christ appeared to him in his usual way.' . . . This vision consoled him, gave him strength, and helped him to arrive in Padua."* How I wish I'd known that story before my traveling companions abandoned me in the dark; I might have turned to Christ—or at least Ignatius—instead of just feeling sorry for myself.

Of course, I wasn't abandoned for long. I caught up with the pilgrims at the base of the Cervera walls, where they had gathered to begin the day's prayer. Beckoning to Porter, I rested my head against his shoulder, whispering, "Please don't leave me alone this morning!" He stuck by me like a bodyguard from that point. Even with his help, it was hard going over rocky ground in the dark. God bless Betsy, who tossed me her headlamp. Since Porter and I continued to trail the pack, her kindness probably spared us a twisted ankle.

Still, it was quite beautiful, watching the last stars disappear and the sky turn all kinds of lovely colors. Soon enough, the painkillers kicked in. As the sun was on the brink of rising, we passed through the tiny village of Vergós, where we were greeted by a friendly dog—a black lab named Rufo—who escorted us through town. He kept running ahead, turning around to make sure we were following, and barking his encouragement. Apparently, Rufo is a regular along the Ignatian Way; Veronica remembered the same furry trail angel escorting her six years earlier, and Fr. José said that sometimes Rufo accompanies the pilgrims so far they have to phone his owner to come drive him home!

At one point, our route crossed a deserted highway and disappeared into some trees. As Porter and I crossed, we saw that Fr. José had stopped to wait for us. He beckoned us over. *Dagnabbit!* He was going to take me out of the game; I could feel it coming. I braced myself, prepared to hear him say, "Wait here for a taxi." But instead, he peered down the highway and said, "Go straight on this road. Roundabout. Bridge. Bus stop. Wait for us!" I asked him to repeat the instructions and he did, then waved goodbye. So off we went, just the two of us.

It was spectacularly refreshing to be alone, walking at our own pace on a paved surface, but it was equally refreshing to be together. In general, we hadn't walked in tandem—both because we were connecting with other pilgrims separately and because Porter had been trying to stay near the front of the Slinky to get some rest during the breaks. (When we returned home, my brother confessed to worrying that we'd been fighting, as we never appeared near each other in the photos that showed up on social media.) But only the previous day, Porter had mentioned that he often felt lonely on the trail, neither keeping up with the rabbits nor hanging back with the turtles. "That's such a shame," I said, "because I'd love to be walking along having a good conversation with you!" Suddenly, there we were, watching the sun come up as we walked together along a quiet road. And we did, indeed, have a memorable conversation, unburdening our hearts in a way the pressured schedule had not permitted earlier.

Reaching the bus stop in Sant Pere dels Arquells, we aired our feet, adjusted our bandages, and retied our boots. When the group arrived, they were shocked to see us looking so happy. That bit of private respite was all we had needed to be engaged for the rest of the journey. I felt like Elijah, strengthened by an angelic meal to walk forty days and forty nights to the mountain of God. Nevertheless, after lunch at the ten-mile halfway point, we took a taxi to the next pilgrims' shelter. Tomorrow we would walk to Montserrat; I wasn't doing anything to jeopardize that dream.

Emailing with Fr. José at Christmas, I thanked him again for the gift of a shortcut that day, telling him how meaningful it had been for me. He responded, *You know, God is always giving directions, and if we are ready to hear, then miracles happen! That day, walking to Jorba, I got the call saying, "Listen . . . we should do something to ease the pain" . . . and that was all!*

I love the image of Fr. José "getting the call" to help me—and I'm so glad he answered!

What can you do to ease someone's pain today?

CHAPTER THIRTY-FIVE

An Easier Way

*Now to him who is able to accomplish far more than all we
ask or imagine, by the power at work within us,
to him be glory in the church and in Christ Jesus to all generations.*

—Ephesians 3:20–21 (NABRE)

That shortcut on the road from Cervera lingered in my prayer, and I tried to figure out why it had been so profoundly moving. I finally realized that Fr. José's personal kindness had felt like a divine intervention. José noticed how much I was struggling, understood that I wanted to press on, and cared for me enough to find a way. I felt seen, known, and cherished—by him, and through him, by God. I gave thanks for that for a while, then dug deeper. If God was communicating, what was the message? It struck me that, through Fr. José's offer of a shortcut, God had said, *You know, there's an easier way to do this.*

Well, that was intriguing. With only one week to go on the Camino, I had begun thinking about the life and work I was returning to. The questions that had been with me from the beginning still needed answering. In the autumn of my days, how was God calling me to use my remaining strength, health, and resources? What inordinate attachments threatened my ability to respond generously?

The whole pilgrimage had been inviting us to walk in freedom, to move more lightly in this world, and to think of ourselves as being always on mission with Jesus. Increasingly, I had the sense that God was not finished with me—that I wasn't coasting into any cozy retirement but gearing up for more meaningful work. Yet, I was resistant. My writing and public speaking need to be grounded in prayerful reflection; this requires a certain spaciousness of mind and heart. Working to deadline is hard enough; *praying* to deadline is ridiculous! Nothing in me wanted to return to my old calendar-scheduled-to-the-margins lifestyle, which I blamed for the way my legs had shut down four years earlier.

But God had said, *There's an easier way to do this.* With a jolt, I realized how often I make life harder for myself by insisting on doing things a certain way, like searching for the "perfect" graphic for a handout destined for people's recycling bins (or—ahem—coordinating everyone's travel arrangements to Loyola). Though I am very good at complicating what should have been a simple task, I'd just been handed a new operating principle. Now, I had to figure out how to apply it.

I resolved to be on the lookout for God's invitations to simplify both what I choose to do and how I choose to do it. Throughout the pilgrimage, my understanding of my mission had been crystalizing into one phrase: *Put it into words.* Put into words God's love . . . God's mercy . . . God's continuous, transformative, tender beckoning. Those words could be written, spoken, sung, or even embodied in acts of kindness. What mattered was that I limit my "yes" to choices in keeping with that mission and focus on its essence rather than frilly complications. Then, indeed, God's power at work in me could accomplish far more than all I asked or imagined.

I shared this insight in my Christmas email to Fr. José, and he affirmed it vigorously. When giving retreats, I mentioned, I want to be more open to where the Spirit leads, rather than spending hours scripting out every remark. José responded, *The tension is between to do a very good, almost perfect speech, or to give a nice speech that is more open to whatever could come from the audience . . . Your strength is the Lord . . . He is the Word you need.* Once again, I felt seen, known, and cherished.

The day of the shortcut ended at a pilgrims' hostel in Jorba, a comfortable establishment (as rooms full of bunk beds go) run by a diocesan priest who serves as both innkeeper and head chef. Before dinner, we gathered at a table running the length of the sun porch, and Fr. José led us in an Examen of sorts, asking each of us to name something we were grateful for and something we were sorry for. The sharing was vulnerable and heartfelt, sealing the fruits of the Camino.

Tomorrow, we would journey at last to the place that had been Iñigo's destination all along: the Sanctuary of Montserrat.

Might God be inviting you to simplify something in your own life? How will you respond?

WEEK FOUR:

SHRINES

MONTSERRAT ~ MANRESA ~ BARCELONA

Take and Receive

The Suscipe *(Latin for "receive" or "accept")* is Ignatius's great prayer of surrender, offering his whole being to God. This utter relinquishing is only possible for someone who has profound trust in God's goodness—a trust that Ignatius believed would be the logical response of anyone who completed the Exercises.

Intriguingly, current Jesuit scholarship suggests that a more faithful translation of the penultimate line would not be "Give me only your love and your grace," but rather, "Grant me only to love you; give me this grace." We do not need to beg God to love us. The sufficient grace Ignatius desires for us is the ability to love God—a love that should consist, he says, in deeds more than words. While the current phrasing anchors several beloved musical settings of the Suscipe and therefore is unlikely to be changed any time soon, it is worth praying the alternate language to sense the difference. Imagine needing nothing beyond the grace to love God!

IN HIS OWN WORDS:

Take, Lord, and receive all my liberty,
my memory, my understanding, and my entire will—
all that I have and call my own.
You have given all to me.
To you, Lord, I return it.
Everything is yours; do with it what you will.
Give me only your love and your grace.
That is enough for me.

—*Spiritual Exercises of Saint Ignatius Loyola #234*

CHAPTER THIRTY-SIX

Ascent

They that hope in the LORD will renew their strength,
they will soar on eagles' wings;
they will run and not grow weary, walk and not grow faint.

—Isaiah 40:31 (NABRE)

Because our journey to the mountains of Montserrat would unfold in stages with varying levels of difficulty, Fr. José advised the pilgrims accordingly. Two women recovering from recent knee surgery decided to go with the luggage vehicle straight to the monastery, while three others accepted a ride to a rendezvous spot just beyond the most strenuous part of our ascent.

The rest of us caught a local bus from Jorba to Igualada—a significant place in the story of Ignatius. There, according to his *Autobiography,* he had purchased a "poorly-woven piece of sackcloth, filled with prickly fibers." From this, he made the simple pilgrim's garment into which he would change at Montserrat, signifying his new way of life. In Igualada, we switched to a larger bus, one that would drop us off at the beginning of our twelve-mile ascent.

I was conscious of how much my attitude had shifted since Arantzazu: I *wanted* the experience of a challenging climb. My blisters were down to a dull ache; my legs felt strong, and my spirit was glowing. Speaking about *The Way,* Martin Sheen once described pilgrims as "seeking to unite the will of the spirit to the work of the flesh." This is what that day felt like for me. We were climbing to the shrine upon which Ignatius had set his sights when he left Loyola, determined to lay down his sword and dagger at the feet of Our Lady of Montserrat. I wanted to feel his striving in my bones.

Our route ascended steadily along a narrow road and then a dirt path. As we topped a rise, we caught our first glimpse of the magnificent, serrated mountains of Montserrat. Every cell phone came out as we stopped to take pictures. "The mountains look like hands praying," Fr. José observed. Getting back onto a road, we traversed a suburb where it seemed every home was guarded by a barking dog; their discordant chorus accompanied us as we walked. At the edge of Sant Pau de la Guardia, we reached a picturesque inn with outdoor seating. Lining up our backpacks and hiking poles on the patio, we went into the bar to grab an invigorating *cortado*.

Finally entering the natural park surrounding Montserrat, we began to climb the forested trails. There was a brief but adventurous descent, as the path crossed some large boulders with a drop-off too steep to step down. Again, my attitude stayed buoyant—*Okay, let's figure out how to do this*. Tony, Charlie, and Carmen snapped into action, jumping down then passing the women's backpacks and walking sticks like a bucket brigade so we could move unencumbered. Gripping us firmly, one by one, they helped us to safety.

An hour later, we emerged onto a real road—the one that carries day-trippers in tour buses—where we greeted the pilgrims waiting patiently for our arrival. Montserrat's distinctive mountain ridges now towered above us to the right, while the river valley spread below us on the left. Fr. José invited us into prayerful silence once more. (Besides helping us approach our sacred destination more meditatively, going single file reduced the odds we'd be clipped by one of those big buses.)

I turned my mind to the concept of humility—the topic for the day in our pilgrim's workbook. As I pondered the challenges of the past few weeks, I realized something unnerving. Though I had received much help, I had *asked* for very little. Usually, I just struggled along until someone noticed and responded, generously. Needing so much assistance might have felt humiliating, if my fellow travelers hadn't woven such a soft blanket of compassion between me and the ground. In prayer, I surfaced those memories like a slide show: Mama Jane carrying my backpack . . . Canada Jane giving me her flip-flops . . . Tony matching my steps on a difficult ascent . . . Ann loaning me her hiking poles . . . Betsy tossing me her headlamp. So much uncalled-for generosity—literally un-called-for. In my journal that night, I wrote, *Being offered help is humbling, but* asking *for help takes humility, and I feel like I've not been very good at that.* I still had so much to learn.

Eventually, we came to a grassy opening with picnic tables outside the restored tenth-century Church of St. Cecilia. We rested for a while, feasting on the sandwiches the priest-innkeeper at Jorba had made for us. Prying off my boots, I discovered that one of my bandages had become unmoored and was no longer protecting its blister. Without even thinking, I shouted, "Hey, does anyone have medical tape?" (How about that: I asked for help!)

We continued along the road for another hour, passing through tunnels cut into the mountains. Finally, Fr. José led us across the road and pointed to some stairs carved into the rock; apparently, we had one more challenging bit to go. Though we could have continued along the winding road, this last climb undoubtedly shortened our steps.

At the top of the ascent, a gate led to a paved path where the pilgrims were gathering—and singing! Tony and Dave were working out the harmonies to "Dona Nobis Pacem" ("Grant Us Peace," a gorgeous three-word canon often sung as a round). I joined my soprano voice to Dave's bass and Tony's tenor, and for a few moments we dwelled out of time, aches and exhaustion forgotten, suspended in the divine peace the song invokes.

Once everyone reached the path, we walked together along the Way of the Magnificat, named for the many mosaic works of art depicting lines from Mary's Canticle at the beginning of the Gospel of Luke. We rounded a corner and then—behold—the plaza of the great Benedictine Monastery of Montserrat.

Recall a time when you were striving to reach a goal. As you hold that memory in prayer, can you imagine God renewing your strength, helping you "soar on eagles' wings"? What challenge lies ahead of you now? Can you pray with Isaiah, "They that hope in the LORD will renew their strength . . ."?

CHAPTER THIRTY-SEVEN

Monastery

Rejoice always. Pray without ceasing.
In all circumstances give thanks.

—1 Thessalonians 5:16–18 (NABRE)

Spending two nights at Montserrat was like visiting the Magic Kingdom. The vast complex houses a monastery, basilica, museum, and library, a fancy hotel and an excellent hostel, as well as several restaurants and gift shops. Funiculars carry visitors up and down the mountain, while buses and trains from Barcelona run full- and half-day excursions; the bustle subsides in late afternoon when the last one pulls away.

We stayed in the hostel, a modern building with an amenity we hadn't experienced anywhere else: washers *and* dryers. Each room had three sets of bunk beds built into the walls, with ample storage and two bathrooms—one with toilet and sink, the other with sink and shower. Although Fr. José would have been within his rights—and, more importantly, his budget—to pack six of us into a room, he must have known we needed a break from the intensity of the last few days. It would be bottom bunks only for the next two nights! I was standing with Rose and Karen when he handed out keys, so we got to bunk together like the college roommates we'd never been.

Several hikes were available during our free day, as Montserrat is a destination for outdoor enthusiasts as well as religious visitors. Fr. José offered to escort people to a far-flung chapel for sunrise, and/or lead a ninety-minute climb to the very peak of Montserrat. A few joined him at dawn, but no one took him up on the longer expedition. Personally, I resolved for the next forty hours not to go anywhere I couldn't wear those hot pink flip-flops.

Despite the magnificent vistas surrounding it, the Basilica itself has a magnetic appeal. Bells ring out periodically, calling people to prayer. The present Basilica is more recent—and far grander—than the original church, but the Benedictine community dates back to the eleventh century. The monks had been there for almost five hundred years when Ignatius made his pilgrimage five hundred years ago!

We visited the Basilica several times during our brief stay. On the first day, we participated in the monks' Evening Prayer—one of the seven daily periods of communal prayer that comprise the Liturgy of the Hours. As they chanted the appointed psalms, I was moved by the sense of having dipped for a moment into the great river of prayer that runs through the Benedictines' days. The following afternoon, we heard a concert of sacred music by the famous Montserrat boys' choir—the *Escolanía*. The music was ethereal, and the expressions on the young faces captivating. We also attended Mass at the Basilica, where we were startled to see Fr. José amidst the monks in the sanctuary—and more startled to see him escorted to the high ambo after the Gospel was proclaimed. (Mass was celebrated in Catalan; for the sake of the Ignatian pilgrims, the monks had invited José to re-read the Gospel in English.)

During that Mass, I felt a rush of closeness to my mother as I thought about how much she would have loved being at the Basilica. A high school theology teacher for most of her life, Mom had been a European history major in college, yet she never crossed the pond—never got to see the marvelous places about which she had studied and taught. I was hit with a familiar wave of sorrow that she had traveled so little before her death at age sixty-seven. But just as rapidly, the strongest sense of her presence washed over me. Tears of joy leaked down my cheeks. Mom did not get to experience these places in her lifetime, but I truly believed she was seeing them through my eyes now.

At the heart of the Basilica is the statue of Our Lady of Montserrat, situated high above the main altar. A twelfth-century carving whose origins are shrouded in mystery, the statue is sometimes referred to as *La Moreneta* (the little dark one). Mary sits enthroned with Jesus on her lap, holding a globe in one hand and resting the other on the child's shoulder. Baby Jesus raises his right hand in blessing, holding in his left a pinecone—a symbol of eternal life. Their robes are bright gold and Mary's veil colorfully decorated, but—like other "Black Madonnas" throughout the world—their skin is strikingly dark. No one seems to know why; it could be an artistic decision or the natural effects of time. What we do know is that *La Moreneta* has captured the imagination of generations of pilgrims—including Ignatius himself.

On March 24, 1522, Ignatius resolved to keep an all-night "vigil of arms" before his Lady of Montserrat. Five hundred years, seven months, and five days later, we prepared to keep a vigil of our own.

———————————

Call to mind someone you have loved and lost. Can you imagine that person seeing the world through your eyes now? What experiences would you most like to share with them?

CHAPTER THIRTY-EIGHT

Vigil

My eyes are awake through the night watches,
that I may meditate on Your word.

—Psalm 119:148 (NKJV)

During our full day at Montserrat, two of the pilgrims arrived, breathless, to an appointed rendezvous. "Sorry to be late," they said. "We were trying to go visit the statue, but the line was too long." Fr. José's eyes twinkled, even as he shook his head. "That line is for tourists," he said. "You are *pilgrims*. We will spend time with her tonight."

At nine-thirty—arguably bedtime—we gathered in the courtyard of the Basilica. A monk appeared, beckoned us in, then re-locked the heavy door and escorted us down a long hallway running the length of the darkened church. Reaching the front, we ascended a twisting staircase and emerged in front of the statue of Our Lady of Montserrat. For someone called "the little dark one," she's bigger than I imagined— about three feet tall, seated. "Just say hello," Fr. José said. "We'll be back." Descending the staircase on the other side, we entered a small chapel, where the statue can be seen through a window above the altar. There we would keep our vigil.

Since reading Ignatius's *Autobiography* in college, I'd had a mental image of his "vigil of arms." I knew he'd had his sword and dagger placed in front of the statue, signifying a rejection of his former way of life, and that he'd stayed awake all night, alternately standing and kneeling. However, I'd always pictured him alone, which I was surprised to learn was wildly inaccurate. I didn't realize that Montserrat was a popular pilgrimage destination even then, or that he'd done this on March 24th—the eve of the Annunciation, a significant feast of Mary. The future saint had not kept a solitary vigil; rather, Fr. José described a packed chapel choked with the smoke of candles and oil lamps and the stench of other penitents.

As with all the significant shrines we visited, the church where Ignatius prayed has long since been destroyed and rebuilt, but the statue itself has remained intact through the centuries. I found it hard to take my eyes off her, knowing that Ignatius had gazed upon this very object all through his long night of prayer. To be clear, neither of us was "worshipping" the statue. That fascinating carving simply focused our attention on the Blessed Mother, who, in turn, pointed us to her Son. To emphasize that, our prayer during the vigil took us through the Stations of the Cross from Mary's perspective. We contemplated the arrest, condemnation, and execution of Jesus as narrated by his mother, an emotional experience that connected us to heartbroken parents throughout the world.

Incidentally, we had one extra companion for our vigil. After the gates closed behind us, we discovered that a Spanish tourist had slipped in, not realizing that ours was a private audience. Unbothered, Fr. José invited the woman to sit next to him, and pulled up the translation of our prayers on his phone so she could follow along. Such gracious hospitality!

As the vigil drew to a close, its key moment lay before us. Several days ago, Fr. José had invited us to begin thinking about a question: What could each of us relinquish as a symbol of our desire to be permanently changed by this pilgrimage? Ignatius had laid down his weapons of war at the feet of the Virgin. Whether we brought an object to leave behind, as he had, or simply wrote our intention on a piece of paper, Fr. José encouraged us to get specific about the conversion we sought.

Long before I knew we were going to reenact this part of Ignatius's pilgrimage, the question of what to "lay down" at Montserrat had been on my mind. What did I want to shed my attachment to? I remember talking about it with Fr. Jim Fleming before the commissioning, confiding that it was already weighing on me, this trying to figure out what to release to God. "What about memory, understanding, and will?" he quipped. (He was referring to Ignatius's great prayer of surrender, the *Suscipe*, which begins, *Take, Lord, and receive all my liberty, my memory, my understanding, and my entire will.*) "Very funny," I groaned, yet we both knew he wasn't kidding; such freedom really is the goal. My brother had even alluded to it on a summer bike ride, when I confided how excited I was by the prospect of being profoundly changed in some way by the Camino. "Remember," Stephen warned, "according to Ignatian spirituality, the expectation of change is one just more thing to let go of!"

More than a thousand years before Ignatius kept his vigil, St. Augustine wrote, "God is always trying to give good things to us, but our hands are too full to receive them." I had no doubt that God desired to pour new life and fresh grace into me as a result of my pilgrimage, but I was going to have to clear some room in the storehouse of my soul.

That night at Montserrat, I parted with a small symbol, one I am continuing to ponder. I decided to leave behind the lavender-scented eye mask I'd shoved into my suitcase at the last minute. The mask was both heavy and impractical; having no strap, it could only balance on my eyes for the first few minutes of each night, until I rolled over. What a waste of space and weight! I decided to leave it at the feet of Our Lady of Montserrat as a sign of my desire to release my attachment to physical and emotional comfort.

Fr. José had placed a gift bag in front of the statue. One by one, we filed back up the stairway, giving each person time to linger in prayer before placing their object or slip of paper in the bag. (We were not alone in this practice of devotion; apparently there is a room at Montserrat where relinquished items are kept before being donated or discarded.) When my turn came, I prayed to be freed from any desire for comfort that keeps me from doing God's will in my life. Writing about it in my journal afterward, I added, *Jesus, please keep showing me what you want me to leave behind (sharp tongue, judgementalism, etc.) so that I can live lightly and joyfully in your service.*

What did the other pilgrims place at Mary's feet? Surprisingly, most people kept that information to themselves, despite our many long conversations and general lack of privacy. Those who did share identified poignant surrenders: grief; worry; the need to be "right"; barriers that keep inner light from shining; negativity; gloom. One person wanted to lay down a tendency to try to control things and strengthen her faith in the slow work of God. Another left a palm-sized rock symbolizing a desire to be freed from making snap judgments. Apparently, that little bag had held some big attachments!

It was approaching midnight when we said goodbye to the Virgin of Montserrat, craned for one last glimpse of the sacred basilica, and heard the bolt clang behind us. We gathered around Fr. José to get our marching orders for the morning, attracting the attention of a security guard on a Segway who hastened to disband us like unruly teenagers. Trying to appear chastened (yet giggling softly), we made our way across the courtyard and back to our rooms, grateful that breakfast in the cafeteria wouldn't be available until eight o'clock.

It had been a late night, and the road to Manresa was long.

Is there something you need to let go of in your life right now? What object might symbolize that change? Can you place it somewhere as a sign of your desire for permanent transformation?

CHAPTER THIRTY-NINE

From the Rising of the Sun to Its Setting

From the rising of the sun to its setting
let the name of the LORD be praised.

—Psalm 113:3 (NABRE)

The sun had barely peeked over the horizon when we gathered in the plaza of Montserrat to begin the last leg of our journey. With the mountains and monastery behind us, we stood for a moment, gazing across multicolored clouds that blurred into the hazy landscape below. This might be the most dazzling spot on the whole Camino, yet we could not linger there if we wanted to reach Manresa by sunset.

We picked our way down the steep path we had climbed two days ago, crossed the road, and began to retrace our steps. Suddenly, a call rang out: *Stop where you are!* Near the end of the line, Liz had fallen by the guardrail, landing awkwardly on her wrist. There wasn't room for us to gaggle around her safely, so Fr. José halted the group, then snapped into action. Though the rest of us were trying to travel lightly, that man had to be prepared for every emergency; he whipped out his medical supplies and taped up Liz's wrist right there on the side of the road. (In retrospect, it is astounding that twenty-five middle-to-older-age adults of varying fitness levels sustained only one injury all month. I hope our guardian angels got paid overtime.)

Reaching the picnic tables at St. Cecilia's, we changed course and began working our way down the other side of the mountain, traversing rocky switchbacks for three hours. Fr. José pointed out prickly little red fruits on what he called a "strawberry tree" (*arbutus unedo*, I later learned), and urged us to enjoy some of the bright berries. Though difficult, this segment of the hike was both beautiful and exhilarating. I remembered how challenging it had been descending out of the Cantabrian mountains three weeks ago, but this felt different. The trails were dryer, but also, I

153

was stronger and more confident. All that hiking, so many days, step by step, and here we were, walking the last miles to Manresa.

Interestingly, we were headed north for the first time. Although Ignatius had been bound for Barcelona when he left Montserrat, he did not want to go by the main road, fearing he might be recognized. Even in his rough garb, his distinctive appearance and courtly bearing could reveal him as the "Loyola" of his former life, and he was determined to travel as a poor, anonymous pilgrim. So he took a circuitous route via the town of Manresa, where a few days' rest would turn into eleven months of soul-searching.

Our assigned prayer for the morning was the *Exercises'* "Contemplation to Attain Love." In it, we consider all the blessings of our lives—no short list—and imagine how God works in and through all creation (including ourselves), sustaining everything with infinite power, goodness, and mercy. At each turn, we consider what the appropriate response to such lavish love might be. Keeping in mind Ignatius's insight that "love should be expressed in deeds more than words," we reach the conclusion that our response should be nothing short of a complete gift of ourselves to God: *Take, Lord, and receive.*

As the Contemplation to Attain Love is a high point in the *Exercises*, Fr. José let us continue far longer than the usual two hours; we did not break silence until almost twice that time had passed. (I never discovered whether that was intentional, or he simply needed a break from the large group's endless chatter.)

Eventually, we left the natural park and entered a neighborhood, the sound of barking dogs reminding us that we were once again in "civilization." Civilization, we realized, might mean lunch, so we perked up, anticipating an oasis. At about two o'clock, we reached a small restaurant in the town of Castellgalí. We took our seats around long tables in a partly shaded courtyard, grateful to be off our feet. Fr. José had placed an order the day before; now he bounded back and forth from the kitchen, calling out names of sandwiches and delivering them to our table. Once everyone had a beverage (non-alcoholic; we'd all learned *that* lesson), we raised a glass. Charlie said I got the "most-improved pilgrim" award, which made my heart sing. I was proud to be doing so much better it showed—though that sentiment betrays a certain lack of Ignatian indifference!

As pleasant as it was to linger there, our step-counters told us we had at least five miles left to walk, so we began to stir. Fr. José looked amused. "What are you doing?" he asked. "It is not time to go yet." He directed us to the novelty ice cream freezer inside, inviting us to help ourselves. "Show the bartender what you took, and he'll put it on the tab." What a guy! There is no way *frozen treats* were a necessary Camino expense, but I'm sure he knew we could use an extra shot of energy for the hot miles ahead. (And, since it was our last hike, there could be no expectation of a repeat offer.) I savored every bite of my vanilla ice cream topped with nuts in a chocolate-lined cone.

Resuming our walk, we turned to see the Montserrat range on the horizon behind us. The mountains looked like a cardboard cutout at the back of a diorama; it was shocking to realize we'd started our day there. Presently, Fr. José cut a corner, dragging us across a large field. Knee deep in dried stalks and sticky burrs, he reminded us that the Spanish word for pilgrims is *peregrinos*—literally, strangers who walk in the fields. "Now you are true *peregrinos*," he joked. Growing serious, he added, "Let us always be grateful for the people we meet along the way."

Our route turned downhill again along uneven terrain; Fr. José informed us that we were now on the *Camino Real,* the Royal Road that Ignatius had often walked as he went back and forth between Manresa and Montserrat for spiritual direction. Once again, I was overwhelmed with wonder: had Ignatius's own sandal touched this rock? It was also humbling to realize that the battle-scarred pilgrim—who never walked without pain—had "often" taken the journey that felt so once-in-a-life-time arduous to me.

Passing through a forest, we stopped for our final rest break. Suddenly, an assortment of provisions appeared, as people emptied their packs of the goodies they'd been hoarding. It was like our own miracle of the loaves and fishes, only with a variety of protein-rich trail mixes instead! We laughed and sampled each other's treasures, thoroughly at ease in one another's company.

Okay. One more push. I couldn't believe this was our last walk together! I looked around at my dear companions, suddenly conscious of all the conversations we *hadn't* had, ample though our opportunities had been. Realizing exactly how I wanted to spend my final miles, I fell into step with Mama Jane.

She and I have stayed in touch via email and agree that our conversation that afternoon was a great blessing. Neither of us is particularly good at small talk. We would much rather go deep one-on-one, so we seized the opportunity to review the key insights and spiritual movements of the last weeks. We shared our esteem for one another, including my gratitude for her blister-guidance at the beginning and her gratitude that Porter and I had picked up the skill and run with it after that. (A month of mending my feet would have gotten old, she confessed.) Jane surprised me by saying she could sense me going deeper into myself as the journey went on. We talked about our involvement in various ministries back home and speculated how our interior transformation might affect them. Could we each maintain the pilgrim's "wandering mind," she wondered—attentive and open, trusting and hopeful—once we resumed our ordinary lives?

As we continued to walk, Jane fascinated me with an explanation of the poetry-writing workshops she runs in Sydney. (She calls them poetry *hobnobs*—what an awesome word!) Though I could feel every sharp stone in the path through the soles of my boots during that last hour, the conversation with Jane kept my mind on higher things.

Shouts from ahead drew our thoughts back to the present, as our companions caught their first glimpse of Manresa. We gathered at a stone tower called Santa Caterina, a former lookout spot in a field high above the Cardoner River. Silence fell as we beheld that vast city, sparkling in the golden-hour light. The expanse of it surprised me. I knew that we would be staying at the Jesuit Center, built above a cave where Ignatius had often prayed. But where was the cave? To anyone in earshot, I groaned, "I really hope Ignatius stopped on the *near side* of this city!"

Fortunately, he had; three-quarters of a mile ahead of us on the banks of the river stood a magnificent complex: the Sanctuary of the Cave and International Center for Ignatian Spirituality (or what I like to call "Jesuit HQ"). We descended from the overlook and made our way to the stone-arched medieval footbridge that Ignatius himself would have crossed. Fully conscious of the momentousness of what we were about to do, we stepped onto the bridge.

At midpoint, we gazed up at the Jesuit complex and saw figures waving wildly. Because of the difficulty of the seventeen-mile journey, a few of our number had traveled with the luggage van, spending the day at Manresa, and Fr. José had put two others in a cab after lunch. Apparently, our companions had been out on a balcony for hours, watching for us. (One had her camera rolling, so there's a video of our bridge crossing.) Another member of the welcoming committee waved from higher up the building: Fr. Nilson, making good on his promise to see us again in Manresa!

Reaching the far side of the bridge, we found ourselves at the base of a steep driveway. At the top was a long flight of steps, beyond which lay the main entrance. We were not finished climbing, but now it didn't matter; even I ran up those stairs. Rocky summiting the Philadelphia Art Museum steps could not have been more exultant! The friends who had been keeping watch swelled out to meet us; everyone hugged one another and celebrated with high fives and photos.

With the sun as low on the horizon as it had been when we left Montserrat, we gathered for a prayer of thanksgiving, ending with our usual song. We had, indeed, been there to "help each other walk the mile and share the load." Every step of the Way.

In prayer, try to become aware of the love God has lavished on you throughout your life. How do you feel called to respond?

CHAPTER FORTY

La Cova

There [Elijah] came to a cave, where he took shelter.

—1 Kings 19:9 (NABRE)

Entering the Ignatian Spirituality Center felt like coming home, probably because it reminded me of my beloved Wernersville. For Fr. José, however, it really *was* coming home: his rooms were in the building! Though we had three more nights together, he was finished living out of a suitcase. The priest appeared at dinner in a golf shirt instead of one of the three *Camino Ignaciano* tees he'd worn in rotation all month. Everyone knew every stitch of each other's wardrobe; it was shocking to see an unfamiliar article of clothing—and comfy loafers, too.

After being greeted warmly by the front desk staff—and, really, anyone who spotted him—Fr. José took us on a tour of his building: dining room, break room with tea and hot chocolate, meeting room, various chapels, bi-level garden. Our rooms were large, with twin beds, private bathrooms, and cool tile floors. After a late dinner during which I could barely keep my eyes open, I collapsed into bed, especially grateful to have reached Manresa at the end of Spanish daylight savings time. The clocks fell back overnight, rewarding us with an extra hour of sleep.

Before breakfast, we took the elevator to the bottom floor to visit the place I most wanted to see: *la Cova de Sant Ignasi* (the Cave of Saint Ignatius). Go ahead and banish any mental image you have of a cave from childhood spelunking; this was not a cavern reached by stooping down with a flashlight to pierce the dark. The place where Ignatius went to pray and write was one of a series of nooks worn into rock by the Cardoner River through a process called "fluvial erosion." On the approach to Manresa, we had seen other such spaces and learned that, to this day, people needing a bit of shelter sometimes take refuge underneath the overhangs.

Ignatius did not live in the cave; he stayed first in a local hospice and later in the homes of benefactors moved by the sanctity of this strange, diminutive, sackcloth-clad man. He begged for alms (which he distributed to those in need) and spent much of each day in prayer, either at the nearby Dominican church or the more remote chapel of Our Lady of Good Health. He began to have spiritual conversations with people he met, sparking the desire to "help souls" that would shape the rest of his ministry. And yet, he needed privacy to wrestle with his tormented conscience—still afflicted by the sins of his youth.

In the First Book of Kings, we learn that the prophet Elijah took refuge in a cave when he feared for his life. This may have been what it felt like when Ignatius retreated to *La Cova*, so distraught was he by his shameful history. Yet, just as in his cave Elijah discerned the authentic whisper of God, in *La Cova* Ignatius sketched out the basic movements of what would become the *Spiritual Exercises.*

That scooped-out bit of rock is now a tiny, ornate chapel at the heart of the Sanctuary of the Cave. Though the chapel is richly ornamented, the ceiling on one side exposes the original, weathered stone. The Cave is the birthplace of the *Exercises*—which alone would make it worth reverencing. But like the Chapel of the Conversion in Loyola, *La Cova* is a place of suffering as well as grace. During his stay in Manresa, the future saint's scrupulous conscience and extreme ascetic practices drove him to the brink of suicide. Those few square meters witnessed a long agony of spiritual birthing from which Ignatius emerged as a new man— one who understood the profound mercy of God. I believe that is what makes *La Cova* such a powerful place, inviting visitors to enter the cave of their own heart as well.

After a visit to the chapel and adjacent church, we enjoyed a quick breakfast, then walked back down that long driveway to explore "Ignatian Manresa." The city has embraced its role as the saint's "school of the soul" in his formative year. A website celebrating the five-hundredth anniversary of his sojourn there lists twenty-two significant sites. We didn't see them all, but with the help of a tour guide we were able to imagine the town as it was in Ignatius's day and visit some of the places that were dear to him.

At three-thirty that afternoon, Fr. José told us, we were to meet in the garden to walk to Mass at Our Lady of Good Health. We should be sure to wear our boots, he added, and bring our hiking poles. *Oh, good grief,* I thought. *How are we not done with those? And why are we hiking to Mass when there are more chapels than I can count right here in our residence?*

The hour's walk took us through the old town and surrounding commercial district, then onto a rocky path through the fields beyond. I will confess, I was grumpy.

My mood lightened when I discovered that we'd be sharing the road with goats. In the field beside us strode an actual *goatherd*—wearing sandals, carrying a crook, and accompanied by a frisky dog. (A twenty-first-century goatherd, he was also wearing jeans and a camo baseball cap, but still, it was pretty cool.) Close on his heels were at least fifty goats of varying colors and sizes, each sporting a noisy bell. As we hustled forward, the goats followed, kicking up a cloud of dust behind us until our ways diverged.

The surreal goat encounter banished what was left of my petulance. And, of course, the walk was worth it. *Santa Maria de la Salut* is a tenth-century hermitage. Preserved in the entryway is a rectangular slab identified (in Catalan, English, and French) as "the stone where Saint Ignatius knelt down on his visits to this sanctuary."

How is it that a hunk of rock touched by Ignatius's knees has been preserved for five hundred years? Fr. José explained that the ordinary people of Manresa kept Ignatius's memory alive, realizing that they had been in the presence of a holy man. According to Tellechea Idígoras's biography, when the saint's canonization process was opened in 1594—seventy-two years after his sojourn in Manresa—many testified to the lasting impression Ignatius had made on them or on their parents and grandparents. Perhaps that's why he continues to feel so present in this place.

As daylight was no longer being saved, the sun had dipped below the horizon already by the time we finished Mass. We started back at a good pace, hoping to reach the paved roads before dark; nevertheless, we had to navigate the treacherous end of the rocky path by flashlight. At last, we reached the bright Burger King and KFC signs on the outskirts of the city—a sharp contrast to the millennium-old hermitage and timeless goatherd. Like many of the towns we visited, Manresa is a place where the past and present coexist.

After dinner, we gathered for our final reflection. Time was moving too quickly! We had waited so long to be in this place, and now we were already preparing to leave it. How I wished I could linger to absorb the miracle of being there.

Once we were seated, Fr. José asked each of us to share how the pilgrimage had affected us. As people mused their way to an answer, it became apparent that many of us had been speculating how the Camino would translate to life at home.

"I'm still me," more than one person said, indicating that any change would be subtle. But several also spoke of noticing what they called *signposts*, indicators of a direction in which God was calling them in their autumn of life. Things people hoped would "stick" included a newfound closeness to Jesus and Mary, a desire to follow Christ in mission, a commitment to "stepping off life's roller coaster" through daily prayer and silence, and a hope to move more lightly through the world, less burdened by possessions. People spoke of wanting to keep their focus on God, accepting whatever came their way as just another part of the journey. Many of us were intrigued by the possibility of doing more things AMDG: for the greater glory of God. We also recalled humbling experiences along the Way and confessed that we hadn't handled them very well—being embarrassed by our shortcomings or trying to solve problems alone instead of reaching out. And we all knew where we'd been stretched, poked, and prodded.

Veronica, who had been carrying so much grief, described the healing experience of God walking with her through nature, through the reflections of Fr. José, and through the friendship of other pilgrims. Tony spoke of the joy of making his own one of the prayers of Pedro Arrupe, SJ, from our pilgrim's book, earnestly saying to Jesus, "I would like to meet you as you really are." Karen shared that she found herself wanting to be more present to the people in front of her—to really listen and be a channel for God's love. When it was my turn, I said that I felt "stretched and strengthened—closer to God and closer to Ignatius."

There was one thing on which we all agreed: the integration of this experience was going to require time and testing. Fr. José assured us that the fruits of the Camino were still ripening in us. He closed with a blessing: "May God teach you to be pilgrims forever."

What would you identify as a holy place in your life? What makes it holy? Even if you can't return there physically, return in memory, and offer thanks for whatever transpired there.

CHAPTER FORTY-ONE

Intercessions

Have no anxiety at all, but in everything, by prayer and petition,
with thanksgiving, make your requests known to God.

—Philippians 4:6 (NABRE)

Before departing Manresa, we gathered in the Sanctuary of the Cave for a private Mass. It was an intimate setting, barely large enough for our group. On one side, shorter people had to sit next to the wall so taller ones wouldn't bang their heads on the low-hanging rock. Shut one eye to the marble ornamentation, and it wasn't hard to picture Ignatius in that space five centuries ago, pacing and kneeling and praying, wrestling with his demons, and jotting down notes that would become the *Spiritual Exercises.*

On the altar, we placed the prayer requests that our family, friends, and members of the IVC community had shared. While one copy remained safely in my travel wallet, the other had been carried by a different pilgrim each day—tucked in a little plastic bag, which one of the early carriers had thoughtfully provided. The creases in the paper were worn from repeated folding, its edges marked up with additional prayer requests that had come our way during the month.

The experience of carrying those prayers had been unexpectedly moving for many of us. At breakfast almost every morning, the person in possession of the list had asked who wanted it that day, handing it off to the next intercessor. That person would not only carry the document but also make time to read and pray the intercessions. It was interesting to hear how each person went about it. Particularly powerful was the day it was carried to Montserrat by the two women who had to take the transport directly there. Arriving well before the rest of us, Ann and Pat settled onto a bench at a beautiful overlook, where they read the prayers aloud and held each intention in the light.

Perusing the paper before placing it on the altar in *La Cova,* I was struck by how much had happened in the lives of some of these people while we'd been praying for them. In particular, there were several intercessions for a peaceful death for those who had, in fact, gone home to God while we were away. I felt deeply connected to all who had shared their concerns, both the ones I knew personally and those who had begun as just names on a list.

Why had we had carried the cares of our community for three hundred miles? We did it as a tangible reminder that we were not making this pilgrimage for ourselves alone. We were one small part of the Body of Christ: his feet, walking along the Way, and his hands, lifting up other members of the Body in prayer. We were members of the Communion of Saints, traveling in the company of Ignatius, the Blessed Mother, all those who'd made the pilgrimage before us, our own beloved deceased, members of our home communities, the wider Jesuit world, and, ultimately, all God's children everywhere.

What a privilege to walk with and for them.

Who will you hold in the light today?

CHAPTER FORTY-TWO

Finale

The LORD bless you and keep you!
The LORD let his face shine upon you, and be gracious to you!
The LORD look upon you kindly and give you peace!

—Numbers 6:24–26 (NABRE)

How many pinnacles can one journey have? Montserrat and Manresa had been superlative experiences, stunningly beautiful and spiritually meaningful; either could have been our final destination. Yet Ignatius had kept moving and so did we, via bus to Barcelona.

Fr. José's original plan had us staying at a retreat house near the Jesuit residence, but for a reason we never discovered there was no room available, so he put us up in a nice hotel instead. (No one complained; there was a pool on the roof!) We only had a few minutes to check in before heading out to explore "Ignatian Barcelona," but I was delighted to spot a large bathtub in my room. Over the next three days, I foresaw much soaking of tired feet.

But first, let's batter those puppies some more with a five-mile walk through the streets of Barcelona. It could have been worse; at least we started by taking the Metro. Twenty-five people, however, is a lot to wrangle in a foreign subway. We were sharing Metro cards with five rides apiece, passing them back across the turnstiles to the next person. A mix-up left us one ride short, so Fr. José told Porter and Carmen to slide through together—immediately attracting the attention of an armed transit officer, who was not amused. (Fr. José hustled over to give an explanation in Catalan, but I will forever refer to that incident as "the time Porter almost got arrested in Barcelona.")

Once we reached the Gothic Quarter, our tour of Ignatian sites was packed, yet only skimmed the surface. In addition to the weeks Ignatius spent preparing for the next leg of his pilgrimage—on to Jerusalem—he later returned to Barcelona for two years of studies. We saw the corner where he lived in the home of a benefactor on a tiny street now named

Sant Ignasi, and visited the church of Santa Maria del Mar, where he regularly attended Mass. A side altar bears a modern, bronze sculpture of Ignatius with one enlarged hand outstretched; a plaque commemorates the place—strategically located near the door—where he used to beg alms for the poor. Mary got her picture taken in that spot, calling Ignatius the "patron saint of nonprofit administrators."

Quite hungry, we stopped at a cafeteria-style buffet. "Just one more church," Fr. José announced after dinner, walking us around the corner to the Jesuit parish of the Sacred Heart. "There is something you must see here." But upon entering the darkened church, he gasped. "It is gone!" The sword that Ignatius had surrendered at Montserrat ordinarily resides in that church, but it had been moved to the Diocesan Museum for a new exhibit commemorating the five-hundredth anniversary of his conversion. (Fortunately, that museum was on our schedule for the following day.) After a brief discussion about whether to attempt the subway again, we walked the "oh, about half an hour" (make that fifty minutes) back to our hotel.

We had to be up and out early the next morning, but I didn't mind; we were heading to *La Sagrada Familia.* Porter and I had visited Antoni Gaudí's masterpiece basilica years ago on a brief visit to Barcelona, and I was eager to return. It did not disappoint. The architect's breathtaking work was inspired by his conviction that "Nothing is art if it does not come from nature." Columns branch like trees into the soaring ceiling, while sunlight washes in through the stained glass—cool tones on the east representing the morning light, warm ones on the west for the setting sun. In addition to a guided tour, we had reserved seats for the multilingual All Saints Day Mass. Fr. José concelebrated and our own Canada Jane proclaimed one of the intercessory prayers in French.

Too soon, we had to leave that magnificent place to visit the Diocesan Museum near the Cathedral, a thirty-minute walk away. I was not excited about our next stop, but my skepticism was misplaced. Titled "The Transformative Power of a Wound," the exhibit was a collaborative effort of the Archdiocese of Barcelona and the Society of Jesus commemorating the quincentenary of Ignatius's so-called "cannonball moment." We beheld at last the sword he had surrendered at Monserrat, then explored displays about the saint's personal history, the spirituality of his followers, and the apostolic works of Jesuits today. Seeing ourselves as part of that rich legacy was a fitting final stop on our whirlwind tour.

The Camino had been an enormous hourglass, but the last grains of sand were slipping through it. Only one item remained on our itinerary: lunch on the *Ramblas*, Barcelona's vibrant pedestrian thoroughfare. In the cellar lounge of the *Restaurante Nuria*, we found seats around a room-length table for one more midday feast. Two other groups were sharing the space, so it was hard to hear anyone more than two seats away. Fortunately, we outlasted them. Over cups of coffee and Catalan cream we offered our words of thanks to Fr. José, along with a little surprise. Knowing that the Office of the Ignatian Camino had incurred many unexpected expenses on our behalf, the pilgrims had pooled our remaining euros (and/or hit the hotel ATM) to make a collective donation to the ministry. I wish I had a picture of Fr. José's face when he opened a gift box and found it full of cash! Also included was a handmade card we had all signed; on the cover was Betsy's cartoon rendering of the man himself, utterly recognizable in his hiking gear.

No words and no amount of money, however, could adequately convey our gratitude. One by one, we said goodbye to the priest who had become so dear to us since that morning he'd hopped off the bus four weeks earlier. I wrapped my arms around him, and he hugged me back. "I don't know how to say goodbye to you," I said.

A few hugs later, he was gone.

How do you handle endings and goodbyes? Can you think of a person or place it was especially hard to bid farewell to? In prayer, try sitting with both hands upturned in your lap. Imagine that one holds the ache of the loss, while the other holds gratitude for the goodness that once was. What is it like to hold both feelings together?

CHAPTER FORTY-THREE

In Praise of Our
Fearless Leader

*Keep on doing the things that you have learned and received
and heard and seen in me, and the God of peace will be with you.*

—Philippians 4:9 (NRSVCE)

Throughout the month, I'd been sending daily updates and photos to IVC's communications manager so people could follow our journey. I dedicated the last of my *Dispatches from the Camino* to Fr. José, asking, "How can I capture this amazing man in words?" In this book, I surely have tried; a quick word count shows that I've mentioned his name upwards of 150 times already. Still, he deserves his own chapter.

Perhaps the shortest and most accurate thing I can say about José Luis Iriberri, SJ, is that he is a true son of Ignatius. (He even looks like the saint, being of Basque descent and cultivating a bit of an Ignatian beard!) He is intimately familiar with the path Iñigo traversed, pointing out churches where he worshipped, buildings where he conducted business, and hostels where he might have stayed. His knowledge of the Jesuits' founder is encyclopedic; I was impressed by the vast amount of information he shared with us each day—without ever consulting notes—about Iñigo's life, culture, and spirituality.

It is one thing to know about Ignatius, however, and quite another to know Ignatius and to model one's life after him. That is the experience of traveling with this man: the sense of being in the company of one of Ignatius's close companions as he guided us through both the outer and inner landscape of the Camino. He was our spiritual guide, in every sense of the term.

Backpack on, walking stick in hand, he moved like a mountain goat, lightly, over any kind of terrain, knowing every twist and turn of those hundreds of miles—most of which he had marked by hand. But he also knew the contours of our hearts, watching us carefully, listening closely to what we said and didn't say, reading our faces, and offering sage observations. He knew when to encourage a flagging pilgrim, when to offer a bit of respite, when to break the tension with a droll remark, and when to put his foot down if someone's ambitions exceeded their abilities. Though he could grow exasperated with our ridiculousness, he was completely attentive and caring the moment someone manifested a genuine need.

The practical tasks he did on our behalf were staggering, starting with booking (and sometimes re-booking) housing and meals for a whole month. Drawing on his skills as a former staff member at the Ramon Llull University school of tourism, he used his connections along the length of the Camino to arrange meetings with mayors, local experts, and those all-important persons-with-keys-to-the-churches so we could slip in after hours to pray. And clearly, he was adept at first aid—tending to blisters and sprains, and translating for us in pharmacies.

Fr. José seemed at home everywhere: in mountains, vineyards, deserts, and shrines. Like a priestly chameleon, the man who'd been clambering over rocks with a tin of spray paint to freshen the orange arrows looked equally comfortable amidst the monks in the sanctuary at Montserrat and on the altar at La Sagrada Familia. He reminded me of St. Paul's words to the Corinthians: "I have become all things to all people, that I might by all means save some" (1 Cor. 9:22, NRSVCE).

The thing that really helped my understanding of Fr. José click into place was a detail I learned over dinner in Lleida: earlier in his Jesuit career, he'd been a university campus minister. As soon as I heard that, I could see the skill set at work. He knew how to frame our prayer at the beginning, midpoint, and conclusion of the morning silence. He sensed when to gather the group for a check-in about how we were feeling, or when to lead us in a touch of the Examen. He intuited what song to play during prayer to evoke feelings lingering below the surface.

Like a spiritual Zumba instructor, Fr. José deftly switched up the pace as needed, knowing exactly how far he could push us and when it was time to ease up. A few nights in a pilgrims' shelter would be followed by one in a surprisingly nice hotel. A long climb would be met at the top by a cute café. A torturous descent would be followed by rest in a woodsy clearing. A sparse breakfast would be followed by a luxurious one. Again, I thought of Sisters of Mercy founder Catherine McAuley, who wrote that "Comfort comes soon after a well-received trial!" (The ice cream treats on the road to Manresa were a classic example of this.)

Fr. José is an exceptional priest and human being; I count spending a month in his company among the great blessings of my life. Sitting on the roof deck of our final Camino hotel, I thought about how batty it had been for him to attempt this journey with us. I remembered an email exchange shortly before the pilgrimage, when I sent him the final roster with demographic information. "These people are pretty old!" he observed. Indeed, describing us as being "in the autumn of life" doesn't really do justice to the fragile bodies and achy joints of a group whose average age was sixty-seven. Yet in the end, there we were: feet worse for wear but minds overflowing with images, memories, and convictions, our souls transformed in ways that would continue to unfold.

At lunch on the *Ramblas*, I stood to make final remarks, saying, "José, you have taken such good care of us. You have taught us so much, not only through your words but by your example. You have modeled Ignatian spirituality, Ignatian indifference, and Ignatian generosity. If, as Ignatius said, 'love should consist of deeds more than words,' you have loved us very well indeed. You told us at the beginning that pilgrimage can change the world, and we have come to believe that this is true."

I pray that Fr. José and the Office of the Ignatian Camino will continue to persevere and flourish for years to come, changing the world one pilgrimage at a time.

Think of a person you know whose love consists of deeds more than words. How do they show their love? How might you be called to demonstrate your love in action?

CHAPTER FORTY-FOUR

Last Things

And now faith, hope, and love abide, these three;
and the greatest of these is love.

—1 Corinthians 13:13 (NRSVCE)

Rose, Carmen, Porter, and I stood on the sidewalk in front of the *Restaurante Nuria*. "What are you guys going to do now?" I asked.

Rose shook her head. "How should I know?" she responded. "This is the first time since we got here that Fr. José isn't telling us what to do!"

I had to concur; after four weeks, the sudden freedom was disorienting; I felt like a canary reluctant to leave its open cage.

We couldn't keep standing on the *Ramblas*, though, so gradually our group dispersed, wandering off in various directions. Porter and I walked—slowly—back to the hotel for some foot-soaking, followed by a nap that could have lasted until morning.

We were awakened by a WhatsApp message announcing an evening gathering to bid farewell to those who had to fly out early the next day. Too tired to go anywhere—and unaccustomed to making our own plans—the group took over the hotel bar, which was staffed by a lone, alarmed waiter until he called for backup. Over assorted drinks and platters of appetizers, everyone kept switching tables and swapping memories, asking questions like, *What was your favorite town? Meal? Church? Fr. José quote?*

We had two nights left in the hotel, and many of us had booked additional time elsewhere in Barcelona. In the days that followed, some people departed, while others rotated in and out of each other's orbits, visiting local attractions and reading or journaling on the roof deck. (The little pool was too cold for swimming but did wonders for sore feet.) One afternoon, Rose and Carmen joined Porter and me for a visit to Park Güell, Gaudí's planned community that's now a UNESCO World Heritage site. Returning to the hotel, we followed a string of WhatsApp messages up to the roof, where several members of our group were relaxing with a couple bottles of wine and cobbled-together munchies. Rose and I contributed the truly terrible "soft" pretzels we'd purchased impulsively on the road. Why Philadelphians would buy soft pretzels in another country, I cannot explain, but they turned out to go nicely with someone else's blue cheese. (The Camino provides!) Conversation turned to travel arrangements, pending obligations, and the looming mid-term elections at home. All agreed, it was going to be hard to leave.

The next morning, most of us were lingering over the breakfast buffet when Fr. José ambled in! We joked that it felt like one of Jesus's post-Resurrection appearances. Apparently, he'd been in the neighborhood and thought he'd pop over to see us. We were shocked, imagining he'd been sick of us weeks ago. ("Are we your best group?" people had asked near the beginning, and he'd smiled enigmatically. Later, when our various illnesses and incapacitations were keeping the transport guys busy, we began asking, "Are we your *worst* group?" to which he responded, "Well, perhaps not the *very* worst!") It was wonderful to see him—though hard to endure a second round of goodbyes. With a cheerful wave, he was off again.

Months earlier, Rose and I had agreed it would be good for the four of us to spend some time together at the end, processing the experience and savoring our memories before flying home. I'd identified a Marriott property right on the *Ramblas* that I thought would be a lovely place to recuperate for our last two nights, and it was a good decision. On the morning of our final full day, Porter and I made "last supper" reservations at a charming restaurant in the nearby Hotel Neri before catching a bus to the Barceloneta beach.

It was early November, but the sun was warm in the cloudless sky. Sitting on a camping towel, looking out over the Mediterranean, we marveled at the wonder of our life.

Was I ready to go back? It was hard to say. Certainly, I was looking forward to seeing loved ones and friends, communicating in real time instead of asynchronously across a six-hour gap. It would be good to be back at St. Vincent's and to resume our monthly IVC and faith-sharing gatherings. But I knew that the answer to everyone's first question— How was your trip?—would be hard to get into words. We had experienced so much, explored so many external and internal paths. The most significant parts of the journey had been what happened in the silence and among the pilgrims. Understandably, people would be curious about the miles, housing, and meals, but I didn't want to reduce the Camino to blisters, hostels, and tapas!

For a month—and, in a way, three years and a month—I'd been learning what it meant to have the heart of a pilgrim. Now it was time to bring that heart home.

What experience do you find hard to put into words? Who in your life has the patience to listen past superficial details for the deeper truth? Can you be that person for someone else?

POST-AMBLE

NOVEMBER, 2022 TO MAY, 2023

CHAPTER FORTY-FIVE

Pilgrimage Is Life

And remember, I am with you always, until the end of the age.
—Matthew 28:20 (NRSVCE)

When does a pilgrimage end?

If the Camino had been no more than a strenuous month of spiritual tourism, it would have ended with our last group lunch in Barcelona. I would have spent the next few weeks getting together with friends to share the highlights of our adventure, then assembled a photo album of our most glamorous (and humorous) shots. But soon, people would have stopped asking "How was your trip?" and *Camino 2022* would have taken its place on the living room shelf next to *Montreal 2014, New Mexico 2015,* and *Cruise 2016.*

Throughout our journey, we often heard Fr. José exclaim, "Pilgrimage is life!" Those three words were the key to making the Camino a truly transformative experience—and thus, a never-ending one.

Let me return for a moment to the words of Paul Elie that I quoted at the beginning of this book. "A pilgrimage is a journey undertaken in the light of a story." When I decided to walk the Ignatian Camino, I thought the story was the journey Ignatius had made five hundred years ago. I wanted to traverse the miles he had traveled and experience the places that had been so significant to him. On the far side, however, I see that the real story was not about the physical miles, but rather the interior distance Ignatius traveled, releasing his attachments to the worldly ideals that had held him bound and learning to dwell in intimate communion with the God of his heart.

Ironically, although our steps followed his journey from Loyola, Iñigo did not put on his pilgrim's robe until he left Montserrat for Manresa. Everything leading up to that, all those miles we walked, was, for him, preparation for the real pilgrimage: the rest of his life. And so it could be for us. Pilgrimage is life; life can be a pilgrimage—if we live it deliberately.

To be a pilgrim in ordinary life is to realize that we step out each day into the unknown. Who will we encounter? How will we be stretched or challenged? What blessing or loss will come our way? Those circumstantial unknowns open the door of our hearts to deeper questions. Will we be present and attentive? Do we trust that we will find God in the midst of it all? Can we (in my spiritual director's words) let go of all the hopes and musings and imaginings that preceded the reality of what is happening, and open ourselves to the grace being offered *through* the reality of what is happening?

Spanish poet Antonio Machado famously wrote, *"Caminante, no hay camino, se hace camino al andar."* (Traveler, there is no road, you make your own path as you walk.) If we resolve to greet each day with a pilgrim's heart, the pilgrimage has no end.

Still, a *book* about a pilgrimage has to end somewhere. You may rightly wonder if my journey bore fruit; if I'd cut off this account after that last lunch in Barcelona, you'd never know—because *I* did not yet know. On the other hand, I could still be assessing the impact of the Way ten years from now, which seems rather long to wait. So, I've settled on six months. That seems like an appropriate amount of time to get a sense of what from the Camino is going to abide.

Upon our return, the "regular" life we'd held at bay for five weeks came rushing back. It felt surreal. After spending thirty-four nights abroad in twenty-six different beds, I'd wake in my own and struggle to remember where I was. Even my dreams were set in Spain for weeks; close my eyes, and I was back there. My spirit was quietly savoring the experience and trying to discern its lasting effects, but the rest of me had Things To Do.

A whirlwind of catching up with friends and responsibilities quickly delivered us into holiday season, visiting family in Florida for Thanksgiving. In December, I gave Advent programs and sang with the Christmas choir. January was writing month, during which my most productive week was the one I spent dog-sitting my brother's eighty-pound Basset Hound, Hank, who draped himself across the back of the couch like a drooly guardian angel at my shoulder. February and March were marked by travel, as I gave Lenten retreats in New Jersey, Ohio, and South Carolina. April juxtaposed the beauty of singing for Triduum and Easter services at church with the chaos of kitchen remodeling at home. At the end of the month, we drove to Maine to open our summer cottage for the season.

But first, we had an important detour to make, as several of our new Camino friends lived in the Boston area. Six months to the day from when we'd done the Examen together at the pilgrims' shelter in Jorba, Porter and I gathered at Karen and Dave's home with Charlie and Betsy, Beth-Anne and her father—also named Charlie—and Bette and her husband, Bill. (The two non-pilgrims at the table knew what they were in for; to our credit, we did let them squeeze in a few words between our stories.)

With a card table added to accommodate all ten of us in the dining room, the potluck supper felt like a true Camino meal—fittingly accompanied by Rioja Valley wine. It was simultaneously shocking and normal to be in the presence of those amazing people again. Recalling the night we'd met as familiar strangers around that long table at *Ocho Patas* in Barcelona, I decided that our Boston reunion would be a fitting bookend for this narrative.

Over the next two days and several more meals, we reminisced about the pilgrimage and shared from the heart about the lasting effects of our journey. Betsy and Charlie had just returned from a two-week trip to visit their daughter in Buenos Aires; arriving home at three in the morning, they'd discovered that their refrigerator had conked out, leaving them with a smelly mess of spoiled food. They laughed, remembering that a burst pipe in the kitchen had greeted them upon their return from the Camino. "That's it. We're never traveling again!" Charlie joked. But quickly, Betsy observed, "Actually, we're both pretty relaxed about it. Fr. José showed us that none of us knows what will happen next, but we have to trust that it'll be okay." Recalling José's oft-repeated words, "We have God; there's nothing else we need," Betsy said she could see in his eyes that he had absolutely no doubt that anything he needed—rooms in a hotel, a passing car, a meal, arrival before dark—would be provided. His example had helped her grow in trust as well: after the Camino, she'd joined IVC, volunteering three days a week as a teacher's aide.

Karen, too, had experienced a marked transformation following her Camino journey. She shared that she noticed a difference in how she approaches anxiety-provoking situations. Driving to work, for example, she might anticipate a difficult encounter and feel a familiar knot forming in the pit of her stomach. But now, instead of imagining the worst, she asks for God's help, sometimes invoking one or more of the Camino's many Marys to pray for her. Just naming them conjures images of our pilgrim group gathered for morning meditation time, she said, bringing a smile to her face, strengthening her will, and loosening the grip of her anxiety.

Our time in Boston confirmed something I had hoped would be true about the community of pilgrims: we had become a family. I have no doubt, now, that if I showed up on the stoop of any one of their homes, they would throw open the door and welcome me—as I would them. Our WhatsApp thread continues to buzz as people share updates, photos, and prayer requests.

Via email, I've learned of additional transformations that have unfolded in people's lives. Tony reached out to share that his extended meditation on suffering during the Camino had led him to refocus more on the needs of the poor. Once back in Australia, he gathered a group of fellow actuaries to address the way the country's pension system fails those with lower incomes.

"Canada" Jane lost her house along the Ottawa river to a fire, but responded with an equanimity that could only have come from understanding life as a pilgrimage. "It's down to the studs," she wrote, "but no one was injured and no one else's property damaged, so that part is good. As Fr. José would say, it's about where we put our focus." Then she revealed a shocking bit of good news: after a long widowhood, there was a new man in her life. Joy and fear came hand in hand, though, as this new beloved had a heart condition. How could she risk losing someone else? "The Camino taught me to have courage where I find love."

Amazingly, several people soon were drawn to make another pilgrimage: Jim and Evelyn retraced their earlier journeys and walked the whole French route of the Camino de Santiago the following spring, while Dave, Karen, and Liz hiked the Portuguese route for two weeks during the first anniversary of our sojourn. Will Porter and I follow their lead someday? If the Spirit beckons, I pray we will have the grace to answer.

Talking with my fellow pilgrims helped crystallize the key changes I've noticed in myself in the wake of the Camino, centering around *silence, spontaneity,* and *serenity.*

Silence. Although I've always been comfortable with quiet, my appetite for silence has grown; I find myself more hospitable to whatever surfaces from within when I don't surround myself with distractions. National Public Radio no longer provides background chatter while I'm cooking dinner. I don't automatically reach for the car radio button, desperate to fill every nook and cranny of my brain with words. Occasionally, I'll listen to a podcast while doing some mindless chore, only to grow tired of the noise after one or two episodes. I notice that Porter and I can sit in companionable silence more easily; I rarely pepper the quiet with "What are you thinking?" anymore. We've begun going to Quaker meeting for worship when we're able, and I relish being in the company of others committed to the practice of seeking God in stillness.

In this category I will also put my reluctance to re-engage with social media. On the Camino, I focused my communication energies on the photos and reflections I was sending to IVC, but upon my return, I didn't resume my previous level of posting. Even though it might be in my professional interest to maintain an active presence online, I've developed a curious aversion to self-promotion. Perhaps that will have changed by the time I need to market this book; perhaps it will change *because* I need to market this book. But God seems to be inviting me to quiet down, and I'm gladly accepting the invitation. The Camino's two hours of silent prayer every morning, coupled with the lack of electronic diversion for the rest of the day, seems to have cultivated in me a desire for the interior spaciousness that only silence provides.

Spontaneity. After the shortcut en route to Jorba, I reached the end of the Camino intrigued by the insight that there was an "easier" way to do my retreat work. Fr. José's Christmas message continued to resonate: *Your strength is the Lord; he is the Word you need.* This new commitment to Spirit-led simplification was put to the test when Lent began, as I had seven events in four states—almost every talk on a different topic— followed by two more programs during Easter week.

I experienced a qualitative shift. It's not that I went in unprepared (despite the negative connotations of the word *shortcut*). Rather, I went in knowing my material well enough to speak confidently without being attached to reams of notes. With no script to deviate from, I was able to engage my hearers more freely, responding to them, making connections, and sharing inspiration that arose in the moment. It was *fun*. Sometimes it felt like a bit of a tightrope act, but it also felt like God was the pole in my hands and the net spread beneath me. I just had to step out.

Trust and spontaneity began marking my preparations as well. Though occasionally plagued by the notion that I should be planting myself at my desk to bear down on presentations, I don't *have* a desk; I have one end of a high kitchen counter—and that's not where I brainstorm most effectively. Talks simmer on the back burner of my mind for weeks; I stir and season them while out for a walk, or in the shower, or on a long drive. I'm learning that my best work happens when God is ready. And, as I once heard an evangelical preacher say, *God is never late, but rarely early!* Here in the autumn of life, I know I can rely on my daily bread—but I also know it's never coming in Costco-sized loaves.

Serenity. My third big takeaway from the Camino seems to involve being less "flusterable," for want of a better word. The mindset created by walking out the door each morning and taking the day in stride has stayed with me. I often recall the peace that washed over me on the evening that I sat on my air mattress in the Fuenmayor day care center; such serenity, I've discovered, can be summoned in other uncomfortable circumstances if I focus on what I have instead of what I lack. Whether the day—or the week—involves flying around the country giving talks or crawling around the cottage painting baseboards, I have discovered a new willingness to simply be present to the day ahead of me.

Serenity is also a good word to describe my attitude toward the pilgrimage itself. As I caught up with the Boston pilgrims, I found myself wondering what the Camino would have been like if I'd been better prepared. I had taken over 676,000 steps, not one of them without pain. Charlie and Betsy, on the other hand, had not a single blister between them. Imagine all the *other things* they were able to think, talk, and pray about while I was busy dealing with distress and disappointment! I'll confess I felt a pang of envy. But then I realized that, if pilgrimage is life, wishing I'd had a different pilgrimage is as fruitless as wishing I'd had a different life. For better or worse, on the Camino or at home, this is where I am, and this is where God meets me. Right here.

A common bit of writing advice says we should *write the book we want to read*. Nearing the end of these pages, I realize that's exactly what I've done. How better to seal the gifts of the Camino? I've pored over the daily notes I captured with that little Bluetooth keyboard, gazed at hundreds of photos, reread my pilgrim's workbook, and explored the websites of many of the places we visited. Without all those things— especially the notes—I suspect much of the pilgrimage would be a blur of paths, churches, hotels, and blister supplies. I'm so grateful to have a record of the substance of my morning prayers, the conversations I had with my fellow travelers, and the range of emotions I experienced. Immersing myself in these details has allowed me to draw out the insights worth sharing.

In the Christmas cards I sent a month after our return, I tried to capture the essence of what I had experienced, writing: *We returned from the Camino with blisters that will fade, friendships that will not, and an understanding of how to orient our hearts for this pilgrimage we call life. In short:*

· Travel lightly.
· Stay in the present moment.
· Open yourself to the wonder of each encounter.
· Ground your day in prayer, and your prayer in gratitude.
· Rely on (and be reliable to) those who share the journey with you.

The Ignatian Camino taught me how to walk with God, greeting each day with generosity, curiosity, and trust. The six months that followed were varied enough to convince me that these gifts of the Way would endure. It was time to close the laptop.

As Fr. José would have said, *Let's go, pilgrim!*

Reflect on my five Christmas card suggestions for how to orient our hearts for the pilgrimage of life. Which are you already doing? Which would you like to strengthen? What can you practice today to find God along your way?

For Those Who Have Far to Travel

AN EPIPHANY BLESSING

If you could see
the journey whole
you might never
undertake it;
might never dare
the first step
that propels you
from the place
you have known
toward the place
you know not.

Call it
one of the mercies
of the road:
that we see it
only by stages
as it opens
before us,
as it comes into
our keeping
step by
single step.

There is nothing
for it
but to go

and by our going
take the vows
the pilgrim takes:

to be faithful to
the next step;
to rely on more
than the map;
to heed the signposts
of intuition and dream;
to follow the star
that only you
will recognize;

to keep an open eye
for the wonders that
attend the path;
to press on
beyond distractions
beyond fatigue
beyond what would
tempt you
from the way.

There are vows
that only you
will know;
the secret promises
for your particular path
and the new ones
you will need to make
when the road
is revealed

For Those Who Have Far to Travel

by turns
you could not
have foreseen.

Keep them, break them,
make them again:
each promise becomes
part of the path;
each choice creates
the road
that will take you
to the place
where at last
you will kneel

to offer the gift
most needed—
the gift that only you
can give—
before turning to go
home by
another way.

—Jan Richardson

Gratitudes

Without the Camino, there would have been no book, so first applause goes to Mary McGinnity for having a big idea then trusting me to slog through the muddy field of details. Shepherding the process over the next three years, however, would not have been possible without my brother Stephen anchoring the home team. (Thanks for making everything more fun, hon.) And I am deeply grateful—as always—for my spiritual director, Susan Bowers Baker, whose timely counsel about the grace being offered *through* the reality of what is happening continues to anchor my days.

With every book, I rely increasingly on the wisdom of early readers. This time I am so grateful for the pilgrim friends who combed through my manuscript to contribute (or correct) memories: Anthony and Jane Asher, Dave and Karen Hinchen, and our fearless leader, José Luis Iriberri, SJ. Thank you especially to Jane for your treasure trove of quotes, and to Fr. José for straightening out my history and geography. Thank you to Rob McChesney, SJ, for your insights about the spiritually injured Iñigo, to Mary Ellen Graham and Diane Zieg for your sharp eyes and courageous critiques, to Chris Lowney for your encouragement, to my brother-in-law John Green for asking good questions (as always), and to David W. Burns for approaching the manuscript with both a spiritual appetite and a fiction-writer's perspective on plot and pacing.

As I was nearing the end of the first draft, I took an eight-week class in spiritual nonfiction, offered through the Jesuit Media Lab. Profound thanks go to teacher Jonathan Malesic and my classmates for helping me tighten the opening of this book, and to Eric Clayton and Mike Jordan-Laskey for creating such rich, ongoing opportunities for learning and collaboration across the Ignatian world.

This is my third book edited by the incomparable Peggy Moran. Getting to work with you is reason alone to keep writing! Thank you for your enthusiastic curiosity about our journey, which added four thousand words and considerably more color to the narrative.

All these acknowledgments combined would not have this book in your hands if not for the friendship of Jeff Crosby (a fine author and editor in his own right), who facilitated the introduction to Paraclete Press, and for the creative work of Lillian Miao, Lexa Hale, Bob Edmonson, Michelle Rich, and the rest of the Paraclete team. For these surprising soul connections, I am gobsmacked grateful.

Special thanks to Porter for listening to every chapter draft, and above all for walking with me: then, now, and forever.

WORKS CITED IN
FINDING GOD ALONG THE WAY
Relevant excerpt appears beneath citation, along with chapter and page number.

"In His Own Words" excerpts from the Spiritual Exercises:
- •"First Principle and Foundation" p. 40, "Tactics of the Enemy" p. 76, and "Christ the King and His Call" p. 111 are from David L. Fleming, SJ, *The Spiritual Exercises of St. Ignatius: A Literal Translation and a Contemporary Reading.* Institute of Jesuit Sources, 1978.
- •"Take and Receive" (p. 142) is from *Hearts on Fire: Praying with Jesuits,* Michael Harter SJ, ed. Institute of Jesuit Sources, 1983.

Paul Elie, *The Life You Save May Be Your Own: An American Pilgrimage*. New York: Farrar, Straus and Giroux, 2004.

"A pilgrimage is a journey undertaken in the light of a story. A great event has happened; the pilgrim hears the reports and goes in search of the evidence, aspiring to be an eyewitness. The pilgrim seeks not only to confirm the experience of others firsthand but to be changed by the experience.

"Pilgrims often make the journey in company, but each must be changed individually; they must see for themselves, each with his or her own eyes. And as they return to ordinary life, the pilgrims must tell others what they saw, recasting the story in their own terms." – Preface / p. 9

Mary Oliver, "Heavy" in *Thirst*. Beacon Press, 2006.
Surely, God had a hand in this, I muse (mentally paraphrasing a line from Mary Oliver's poem "Heavy"). – Ch 1 / p. 17

Joan Didion, *The White Album*. Simon & Schuster, 1979.
In *The White Album,* Joan Didion described migraines as her body's response to the "guerrilla wars" of her life. Like Didion's headaches forcing her into a darkened room with an ice pack, my legs were shouting that I needed to sit down. – Ch 2 / p. 18

Mary Oliver, "The Summer Day" in *House of Light*. Beacon Press, 1990
To paraphrase Mary Oliver again, we had to ask ourselves: What were we going to *have done* with our one wild and precious life? – Ch 3 / p. 21

Jan Richardson Blessings
"The Shimmering Hours" (excerpt) and "For Those Who Have Far to Travel" © Jan Richardson from *Circle of Grace: A Book of Blessings for the Seasons.* Used by permission. janrichardson.com – Ch 7 / p. 32, Ch 13 / p. 61

"The Servant Song," a song by Betty C. Pulkingham and Richard Gillard (GIA Music)

Before heading to bed, he taught us a customized verse of "The Servant Song," a familiar hymn that became our theme song for the Camino, as we sang it repeatedly each day:

We are pilgrims on a journey;
we're companions on the road.
We are here to help each other
walk the mile and share the load. – Ch 11 / p. 44

"Good King Wenceslas," Christmas carol, lyrics by John Mason Neale to a thirteenth-century tune.

"I'm going to 'Good King Wenceslas' you for a while" she announced on flatter terrain. Immediately, I recalled—in Bing Crosby's rich baritone—the plot of the old Christmas carol. King Wenceslas and his servant walked out on a harsh winter night to bring supper to a poor man. Buffeted by any icy wind, the king made a surprising invitation: "Mark my footsteps, my good page; tread thou in them boldly. Thy shalt find the winter's rage freeze thy blood less coldly." The servant complied: "In his master's steps he trod, where the snow lay dinted; heat was in the very sod which the saint had printed." – Ch 12 / p. 55

Pope St. John Paul II, Encyclical "Solicitudo Rei Socialis" (On Social Concern), December 1987.

Pope St. John Paul II articulated that challenge in his encyclical "On Social Concern" when he wrote, "[Solidarity] is not a feeling of vague compassion or shallow distress at the misfortunes of so many people, both near and far. On the contrary, it is a firm and persevering determination to commit oneself to the common good." – Ch 14 / p. 63

Catherine McAuley, *Retreat Instructions of Mother Mary Catherine McAuley.* Newman Press, 1952.

Reflecting on this abundance of spontaneous kindness, I recalled a favorite quote from Catherine McAuley, the founder of the Sisters of Mercy. "There are three things which the poor prize more highly than gold," she wrote, "though they cost the donor nothing. Among these are the kind word, the gentle, compassionate look, and the faithful hearing of their sorrows." – Ch 18 / pp. 80–81

Jose Ignacio Tellechea Idigoras, *Ignatius of Loyola: the Pilgrim Saint.* (Cornelius Michael Buckley, SJ, trans.) Loyola University Press, 1994.

•In *Ignatius of Loyola: the Pilgrim Saint*, biographer José Ignacio Tellechea Idígoras describes the future saint's early faith as being marked by "imitating the external idiosyncrasies" of the saints who inspired him, "obsessed with notions of *doing* great things rather than enduring or experiencing them." Ch 23 / p. 99

•Months later, I read the following passage in Tellechea Idígoras's biography of Ignatius; it's from the saint's early days in Italy. *"Some of [Iñigo's] traveling companions went off to get a health certificate at Padua. He could not keep up with them because they walked too fast, and so they left him behind 'at nightfall in a vast field.' It was one of his worst experiences of total abandonment, and he tells us that here 'Christ appeared to him in his usual way.' . . . This vision consoled him, gave him strength, and helped him to arrive in Padua."* – Ch 34 / p. 136

•According to Tellechea Idígoras's biography, when the saint's canonization process was opened in 1594—seventy-two years after his sojourn in Manresa—many testified to the lasting impression Ignatius had made on them or on their parents and grandparents. – Ch 40 / p. 160

Ed Caesar, "Only Disconnect." *The New Yorker*, November 29, 2021.
In "Only Disconnect," Ed Caesar narrates having been dropped solo in the remote mountains of Morocco, challenged to use his wits (and GPS) to reach a set destination. The experience—for which he'd paid good money—had been alternately strenuous, frightening, and exhilarating. Only when it was over did he discover that the "Get Lost" support team had been tracking him from five hundred yards back the whole time. Caesar's departure from his comfort zone had been more extreme than ours, but it, too, had balanced uncertainty with security. Though admitting the artifice of what he calls the "luxury of living for a short while under the illusion that I was [disconnected]," he nevertheless found his hike deeply gratifying. As with our pilgrimage, Caesar's external journey had been meaningful only as a catalyst for his internal one. Like us, he did not want the experience to end. – Ch 25 / p. 104

A Pilgrim's Journey: The Autobiography of Ignatius of Loyola, Joseph N. Tylenda SJ, trans. Ignatius Press, 2009.
The rest of us caught a local bus from Jorba to Igualada—a significant place in the story of Ignatius. There, according to his *Autobiography,* he had purchased a "poorly-woven piece of sackcloth, filled with prickly fibers." From this, he made the simple pilgrim's garment into which he would change at Montserrat, signifying his new way of life. – Ch 36 / p. 143

Martin Sheen, interview with *The Washington Post Live*: https://www
.washingtonpost.com/washington-post-live/2023/05/15/transcript-way
-conversation-with-martin-sheen-emilio-estevez/
Speaking about *The Way,* Martin Sheen once described pilgrims as "seeking to unite the will of the spirit to the work of the flesh." This is what that day felt like for me.
– Ch 36 / p. 143

St. Augustine, *The City of God*, 426 CE

More than a thousand years before Ignatius kept his vigil, St. Augustine wrote, "God is always trying to give good things to us, but our hands are too full to receive them." – Ch 38 / p. 151

Antonio Machado, "Caminante, no Hay Camino" in *Campos de Castilla*. Ediciones de la Lectura, 1912.

Spanish poet Antonio Machado famously wrote, *"Caminante, no hay camino, se hace camino al andar."* (Traveler, there is no road, you make your own path as you walk.) – Ch 46 / p. 176

SCRIPTURE CREDITS

Scripture quotations marked (CJB) are taken from the Complete Jewish Bible by David H. Stern. Copyright © 1998. All rights reserved. Used by permission of Messianic Jewish Publishers, 6120 Day Long Lane, Clarksville, MD 21029. www.messianicjewish.net.

Scripture quotations marked (KJV) are taken from the King James Version of the Bible.

Scripture quotations marked (NABRE) are taken from the *New American Bible, revised edition* © 2010, 1991, 1986, 1970 Confraternity of Christian Doctrine, Washington, D.C. and are used by permission of the copyright owner. All Rights Reserved. No part of the New American Bible may be reproduced in any form without permission in writing from the copyright owner.

Scripture quotations marked (NKJV) are taken from the New King James Version®. Copyright © 1982 by Thomas Nelson. Used by permission. All rights reserved.

Scripture quotations marked (NRSVCE) are taken from the New Revised Standard Version Bible: Catholic Edition, copyright © 1989, 1993 National Council of the Churches of Christ in the United States of America. Used by permission. All rights reserved worldwide.

MORE FROM PARACLETE PRESS

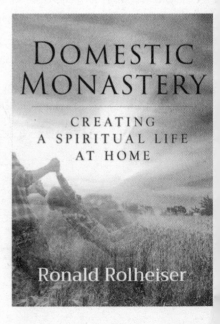